Enriching Children, Enriching the Nation

Public Investment in High-Quality Prekindergarten

ROBERT G. LYNCH

Economic Policy Institute
1333 H Street, NW
Suite 300, East Tower
Washington, DC 20005-4707

www.epi.org

ISBN: 1-932066-28-4

Table of Contents

ACKNOWLEDGEMENTS

This report was made possible by generous support from the Foundation for Child Development, the W.K. Kellogg Foundation, and The Pew Charitable Trusts.

The Foundation for Child Development (FCD) is a national private philanthropy in New York City dedicated to promoting a new beginning for public education from prekindergarten through third grade. The Foundation promotes the well-being of children, and believes that families, schools, nonprofit organizations, businesses, and government at all levels share complementary responsibilities in the critical task of raising new generations. To learn more about FCD and its programs, please visit its Web site at www.fcd-us.org.

The W.K. Kellogg Foundation seeks to help people help themselves through the practical application of knowledge and resources to improve their quality of life and that of future generations.

The Pew Charitable Trusts supported this report as part of its initiative, Advancing Quality Pre-K for All.

The views expressed are those of the author and not necessarily those of the Foundation for Child Development, the W.K. Kellogg Foundation, or The Pew Charitable Trusts.

I benefited greatly from the careful reviews of earlier drafts of this paper by W. Steven Barnett, Donna Desrochers, Rob Grunewald, Lee Price, Arthur J. Reynolds, Art Rolnick, Ruby Takanishi, Fasaha Traylor, and Sara Watson. I am grateful to them for their numerous comments and constructive criticisms. Others who contributed useful suggestions or helped me think through some of the intellectual problems I confronted include Sylvia Allegretto, Jared Bernstein, Josh Bivens, Nancy Coleman, Michael Ettlinger, Elise Gould, Stephaan Harris, Marcia Howard, Louisa Koch, Harold Leibovitz, Edward Lynch, Stephen Lynch, Larry Mishel, Guy Molyneux, Max Sawicky, John Schmitt, and Rob Scott. David Ratner and Kitty Richards provided expert research assistance, collected data, helped develop the methodology, and played a key role in analyzing the data. They also prepared drafts of some sections and provided numerous comments that improved the final document. Michael Ettlinger and Kitty Richards helped to develop the methodology for the extrapolation of the data used in this work. Bella Rosenberg collected and analyzed information about the pedagogy and other factors that account for the success of the Chicago Child-Parent Center program. Noris Malvey played a key role in helping me secure funding for the project. Ellen Levy and Joe Procopio did a wonderful job editing the manuscript. I thank them all.

Any errors and omissions in the book are my responsibility alone.

Executive Summary

Research is increasingly demonstrating that the policy of investing in early childhood development, particularly high-quality prekindergarten, provides a wide array of significant benefits to children, families, and society as a whole. Empirical research shows that all children, regardless of whether they are from poor, middle-, or upper-income families, benefit from prekindergarten programs. In addition, higher quality prekindergarten programs provide greater benefits than lower quality prekindergarten programs.

Children who participate in high-quality prekindergarten programs require less special education and are less likely to repeat a grade or need child welfare services. Once these children enter the labor force, their incomes are higher, along with the taxes they will pay back to society. Both as juveniles and as adults, these children are less likely to engage in criminal activity thereby reducing criminality overall in society. High-quality prekindergarten benefits government budgets by saving government spending on K-12 education, child welfare, and the criminal justice system, and by increasing tax revenues. Thus, investment in high-quality prekindergarten has significant implications for future government budgets, both at the national and the state and local levels, for the economy, and for crime. This study breaks down these benefits at the national level and state-by-state.

This study analyzes the costs and the fiscal, earnings, and reduced crime benefits of public investment in 1.) a *targeted*, voluntary, high-quality prekindergarten education program that serves only three- and four-year-old children who live in families in the lowest quarter of the income distribution, and 2.) a similar, but *universal* prekindergarten education program made available to all three- and four-year-old children. The governmental costs and benefits of both publicly funded prekindergarten programs, measured as year-by-year expenditures, budget savings and revenue impacts, are estimated from program implementation in 2007 through the year 2050. In addition to the long-term budgetary consequences to governments that follow from such investment, the earnings and crime implications for individuals and society are calculated for the same years.

This study demonstrates that investment in early childhood education, even when its benefits are not fully accounted for, is an effective public policy strategy for generating wealth and achieving a multitude of social and economic development objectives. A nationwide commitment to high-quality early childhood education would cost a significant amount of money upfront, but it would have a substantial payoff in the future as such a program would ultimately reduce costs for remedial and special education, criminal justice, and child welfare, and it would increase income earned and taxes paid. Over time, governmental budget benefits alone outweigh the costs of high-quality prekindergarten education investments; that is, high-quality prekindergarten *pays for itself.* Most government expenditures do not create offsetting receipts to the extent that early childhood education does and, indeed, it may be rare to find public programs that pay for themselves at the budgetary level. It is striking that a national program, either funded jointly by federal and state governments or financed almost entirely by the states, will have significant positive effects on the long-term budget outlooks of both federal and state governments. Thus, policy makers should consider a national prekindergarten initiative a sound investment on the part of government that generates substantial long-term benefits and not simply as a program requiring expenditures.

The economic and social benefits from prekindergarten investment amount to much more than just improvements in public balance sheets. Myriad benefits accrue to the affected children, their families, and society as a whole. Children who participate in high-quality prekindergarten programs fare better in school, have better home lives, and are less likely to engage in criminal activity than their peers who do not attend such programs. The participating children go on to higher achievement later in life, graduating from high school and attending college at a higher rate, and earning more once they enter the labor force. Through these mechanisms, investment in young children has positive effects on the U.S. economy by raising incomes, improving the skills of the workforce, reducing poverty, and strengthening U.S. global competitiveness. Crime rates and the heavy costs of criminality to society are reduced, as well. Given that the positive impacts of prekindergarten may be larger for at-risk than for more advantaged children, a universal as well as a targeted prekindergarten program may help to reduce achievement gaps between poor and non-poor children, ultimately reducing income inequality nationwide.

This study estimates that providing a voluntary, high-quality, publicly funded, *targeted* prekindergarten education program serving the poorest 25% of three- and four-year-old children would generate rapidly growing annual benefits that would surpass the more slowly growing annual costs of the program within six years. In the year 2050, the annual budgetary, earnings, and crime benefits would total $315 billion: $83 billion in government budget benefits, $156 billion in increased compensation of workers, and $77 billion in reduced costs to individuals from less crime and child abuse. These annual benefits would exceed the costs of the program in that year by a ratio of 12.1 to 1 (see **Table 1**).

Such a high-quality targeted prekindergarten program would cost almost $6,300 per participant and could be expected to enroll just over 2 million children when it is fully phased in. Thus, the targeted program would initially cost taxpayers about $13.2 billion a year but, with offsets for current commitments to prekindergarten for at-risk children, only an additional $8.2 billion per year, once it is fully phased in. Within nine years, the net annual effect on government budgets alone would turn positive (for all levels of government combined). That is, starting the ninth year and every year thereafter, annual government budget benefits due to the program would outweigh annual

TABLE 1 Budgetary, compensation, and reduced crime benefits of public investment in prekindergarten

Program	Number of years before program annual benefits exceed annual costs	Government budget benefits in 2050 (billions of 2006 dollars)	Increased compensation in 2050 (billions of 2006 dollars)	Savings to individuals from reduced crime and child abuse in 2050 (billions of 2006 dollars)	Total budget, compensation, and crime benefits in 2050 (billions of 2006 dollars)	Ratio of total annual benefits to program costs in 2050
Targeted	6	$83	$156	$77	$315	12.1
Universal	9	$191	$432	$156	$779	8.2

Source: Author's analysis.

TABLE 2 Government costs and benefits

Program	Additional taxpayer costs when fully phased In (billions of 2006 dollars)	Number of years before government annual budget benefits exceed annual program costs	Government budget surplus in 2050 (billions of 2006 dollars)	Ratio of government budget benefits to program costs in 2050
Targeted	$8.2	9	$57	3.18
Universal	$33.3	17	$96	2

Source: Author's analysis.

government costs of the program. Within 44 years, the offsetting budget benefits alone would total $83 billion, more than three times the costs of the program. Thus, by 2050, every tax dollar spent on the program would be offset by $3.18 in budget savings and governments collectively would be experiencing $57 billion in surpluses due to the prekindergarten investment (**Table 2**).

Even if states paid almost all the costs of the targeted program, with the federal government simply maintaining its current commitments to prekindergarten education (redistributing these commitments equitably among states and holding states harmless from potential losses of federal funds), the program would be a boon to state budgets. On average, states would experience net budget savings within 10 years, and by 2050, every dollar spent on the program would be offset by $2.15 in budgetary savings for state governments. These net budget savings would start within as few as four years in Delaware and in no more than 29 years in Alabama. By 2050, every state dollar expended on the program would be offset by at least $1.17 in budgetary savings for Alabama and as much as $4.97 in budget savings in Delaware. And in 2050, the federal government would be experiencing $29 billion in prekindergarten-related budget surplus. Whether funded by states or all levels of government, on top of the budget savings, a targeted prekindergarten program is estimated to increase the compensation of workers by $156 billion and reduce the costs to individuals from crime and child abuse by $77 billion by the year 2050.

A voluntary, high-quality, publicly funded, *universal* prekindergarten education program serving all three- and four-year-olds would produce even greater annual budgetary, earnings, and crime benefits than would a targeted program. The annual benefits of the program would begin to outstrip its annual costs within nine years and would do so by a growing margin every year thereafter. By the year 2050, the annual benefits would total $779 billion: $191 billion in government budget benefits, $432 billion in increased compensation of workers, and $156 billion in reduced costs to individuals from less crime and child abuse. These annual benefits in 2050 would exceed the costs of the program in that year by a ratio of 8.2 to 1.

Such a high-quality, publicly funded, *universal* prekindergarten program would cost nearly $6,300 per participant and could be expected to enroll almost 7 million children when it is fully phased in. Thus, the program would initially cost taxpayers $43.2 billion or, with offsets for current prekindergarten commitments, an additional $33.3 billion per annum, once it is fully phased in. Within 17 years, the net annual effect on government budgets alone would turn positive and by 2050 the budget savings would be $191 billion, double the total costs of the program in that year. Thus, in 2050, every tax dollar spent on a universal prekindergarten program would be offset by $2.00 in budget savings and governments would be enjoying $96 billion in surpluses due to their prekindergarten investment.

If states paid almost all the costs of the voluntary, high-quality, universal program, with the federal government simply maintaining its current commitments to prekindergarten education (redistributing these commitments equitably among states and holding states harmless from potential losses of federal funds), the program would generate budget surpluses in 46 states by 2050. Collectively, states would experience net budget savings with an average budget savings per state tax dollar spent on prekindergarten of $1.26 in 2050. The returns per state tax dollar spent on universal prekindergarten in 2050 would vary by state from a low of 79 cents in Alabama to a high of $1.88 in New York, and the federal government would be enjoying $73 billion in prekindergarten investment-related budget surplus. Regardless of which level of government funds the program, in addition to the budget savings, by the year 2050, a voluntary, high-quality, universal prekindergarten education program is estimated to increase the compensation of workers by $432 billion and reduce the costs to individuals of crime and child abuse by $156 billion. Thus, even if states paid almost all the costs of the voluntary, high-quality, universal program, with the federal government simply maintaining its current commitments to prekindergarten education, the total state benefits of the program would outstrip the state program costs in every state by a minimum of 5.9 to 1 in Alabama and by as much as 11.2 to 1 in Wyoming.

Clearly, investing in high-quality early childhood education programs is an effective public policy strategy that produces a wide array of significant benefits for children, their families, and society as a whole (including its taxpayers). The United States should be investing in high-quality prekindergarten to improve the quality of life of millions of children, make the workforce of the future more productive, strengthen the economy, reduce crime, and provide future budget relief.

Introduction

The ultimate aim of public policy is to promote the wealth of nations, communities, families, and individuals. When determining whether a particular public policy is worth pursuing, it is often useful for citizens and policy makers to weigh the benefits of the policy against its costs. However, it is not always possible to measure or quantify in dollar terms all the costs or benefits of a particular policy.

Public investment in early childhood education is a good example of a public policy whose benefits are difficult to comprehensively and precisely quantify. Public investment in early childhood education that is effective improves educational outcomes, enhances the quality of life of the recipients of the investment, and creates a range of external benefits to society over and above those to individual students. While such investment can increase the knowledge, skills, and literacy of students, it is not easy to accurately measure this improvement in educational outcomes and there is no unambiguous way to translate these improvements into dollar terms. Likewise, while research shows that education is associated with greater levels of life and job satisfaction (Blanchflower and Oswald 2000), it is no simple task to quantify the monetary value of greater happiness. Many of the external benefits to society from public investment in early childhood education, such as the future greater productivity of more educated workers, are challenging to measure, too.

Although not all the benefits from early childhood education investment can be measured and quantified, many can be calculated. The costs of public investment in early childhood education are relatively easier to capture fully and accurately. Hence, the quantifiable benefits and costs can be compared and, even when the benefits are not fully accounted for, such a comparison can inform the public debate on the merits of public investment in early childhood education.

This study analyzes the costs and many, but not all, of the benefits of public investment in the education of children during the early childhood years. More specifically, this study analyzes the costs and the fiscal, earnings, and crime benefits of public investment in 1.) a *targeted* voluntary, high-quality prekindergarten education program that serves only three- and four-year-old children who live in families in the lowest quarter of the income distribution, and 2.) a similar, but *universal*, voluntary prekindergarten education program made available to all three- and four-year-old children. The governmental costs and benefits of both publicly funded prekindergarten programs, measured as year-by-year expenditures, budget savings, and revenue impacts, are estimated from program implementation in 2007 through the year 2050. In addition to the long-term budgetary consequences to governments that follow from such investment, the earnings and crime implications for individuals and society are calculated for the same years. The study demonstrates that investment in early childhood education, even when its benefits are not fully accounted for, is an effective public policy strategy for generating wealth and achieving a multitude of social and economic development objectives.

The process of social and economic development involves accelerating economic growth, increasing incomes, creating jobs, eradicating poverty, tempering inequality, improving education, ameliorating health, reducing crime, providing security to families and communities, and protecting the environment while creating the conditions that enable people to achieve their potential, live lives of dignity, and maximize their choices. Achieving these goals, however, is not easy and the processes that lead to their attainment are difficult to hasten. History and practice have demonstrated that promoting improved living conditions requires a sophisticated and multidimensional approach involving an array of skills, resources, institutions, and policies.

In the United States, many of the ingredients necessary to bring about further economic and social development are already in place. We function along the technological frontier in the fields of science, medicine, and business. Although there are weaknesses, we have a well-developed economic infrastructure of roads, bridges, ports, airports, communication networks, and energy distribution systems. While not limitless or evenly distributed geographically, we have a relatively rich complement of natural resources, from arable land and ample water supplies to abundant quantities of minerals. Over many decades, we have developed quality institutions that support our educational, health care, legal, financial, and political systems. Finally, we have accumulated an impressive stockpile of machinery, equipment, and tools that combined with our large, hard-working labor force give us the capacity to grow rapidly and be more productive in the future.

And yet, relative to our potential, and even relative to some other nations, the United States has fallen short in terms of health and education outcomes, underachieved in terms of economic growth, productivity, job creation, poverty alleviation, equality, and wage growth, and fared badly in terms of crime, security, and environmental quality. Given our strengths in technology, resources, and institutions, the failure to live up to our potential reflects in part the inadequacies of our social and economic policies.

Clearly, no single policy can bring about the rapid and simultaneous achievement of all of our development goals, but just as clearly, policies do matter. And at a time of sharp disagreement over solutions to the many social and economic problems we confront, we should take particular notice when a consensus emerges across the political spectrum on an effective policy solution.

Research is increasingly demonstrating that the policy of investing in early childhood development in general and in high-quality prekindergarten education in particular, has the ability to powerfully impact many of our development goals and positively influence the pace of the development process. Prekindergarten programs provide services to three- and four-year-old children. High-quality prekindergarten education programs tend to have low ratios of children to teachers, small class sizes, and highly paid, well-qualified teachers and staff. In addition, the nature of teacher-child interactions tends to be warm, positive, supportive, and stimulating. Parental involvement is encouraged and cultivated. These programs offer health services and carefully follow safety procedures. The activities in the classroom and the instructional materials vary with emphasis placed on quality instruction in a wide range of fields including art, music, science, math, problem solving, language development, and reasoning. Numerous studies of these high-quality early childhood education programs have found that investing in young children has an array of significant benefits for children, their families, and society as a whole (including its taxpayers).

Early childhood education provides a multitude of benefits to children. In general, children who participate in high-quality prekindergarten programs need less remedial education and special education, and are less likely to require child welfare services. They have higher educational attainment, graduating from high school and attending college in greater numbers. Once these children enter the labor force, their incomes are higher, along with the taxes they will pay back to society. Both as juveniles and as adults, these children are less likely to engage in criminal activity.

In addition to providing clear benefits to the recipients of the program, the effects of high-quality prekindergarten lead to reduced government spending on K-12 education, child welfare, and the criminal justice system, and to increased tax revenues due to a larger tax base. Thus, investment in high-quality prekindergarten education has significant implications for future government budgets, both at the national and the state and local levels, for the economy, and for crime. This study breaks down these benefits at the national level and state-by-state.

Although investment in early childhood education has the ability to positively impact many socioeconomic development goals, such investment has a particularly potent and direct bearing on three areas: the well-being of children, the educational achievement and productivity of children and adults, and crime. All three are areas where we have not only failed to achieve our potential, but also fallen short relative to other economically advanced nations.

The well-being of children

Many young children—the most vulnerable members of our community—have inadequate access to food, clothing, shelter, health care, and clean, safe, crime-free living environments. Though the well-being of children can be analyzed in many different ways, two good indicators are the Foundation for Child Development's (FCD) child well-being index and the official U.S. government statistics on child poverty.

The FCD's child well-being index for American children is a composite of 28 national level indicators in seven quality of life domains including health, education, safety, family income, social relations, emotional well-being, and community connectedness. The good news is that the index hit an all-time high in 2005 (FCD 2006b). However, the 2005 level was only 5% higher than the level 30 years earlier in 1975, the base year. In addition, had the United States maintained its peak levels in each of the 28 components, the index in 2005 would have been about 23% higher than the 1975 base year. Moreover, had the United States achieved levels on the 28 components that equaled the best performance internationally, the index would have been about 38% higher than that of the 1975 base year. Our failure to achieve national and international best practices of the past 30 years indicates that there is substantial room for improvement in the quality of life of our children.

Although the FCD's child well-being index (FCD 2006b) hit an all time high in 2005, it is striking that the index did not show improvement in the area of educational achievement. The math and reading scores of 13- and 17-year-olds, as measured by the National Assessment of Education Progress (or NAEP), were not significantly better in 2005 than they were in 1975. Only the NAEP math and reading scores of nine year-olds showed substantial improvement, which, it is interesting to note, the FCD study associated with the increased availability and quality of prekindergarten programs.

In terms of child poverty, in 2004, 20.2% of all children under the age of six— that is, one out of every five kids, or some 4.8 million children—were living in poverty in the United States[1] (U.S Census Bureau 2004c). About one-fifth of these poor children and nearly 10% of all children lacked health insurance. In a nation that is one of the world's largest food producers and exporters, roughly 17% of all households with children experience food insecurity each year.[2]

The United States fares poorly on child poverty compared to other wealthy nations. Among a sample of 26 relatively rich nations, the United States has the second highest child poverty rate (UNICEF 2005). Only Mexico fares worse. Child poverty rates in the United States are more than double the rates in most other economically advanced countries. Interestingly, variations in policy account for most of the variation in child poverty among rich countries. While public policy reduces child poverty by an average of almost 50% in other rich nations, it does so by only 18% in the United States (UNICEF 2005).

In addition to its effects on the children in question, child poverty is linked to a number of societal ills. Children who grow up in poverty mature into adults who are more likely to engage in crime, have substance abuse problems, abuse and neglect their own children, and suffer from poor health. Poverty also has a tendency to reproduce itself: children in poverty are more likely to live in poverty as adults and have children who will then grow up in poverty.

The educational achievement and productivity of children and adults

Many American children, whether they come from poor, middle-income, or wealthy families, do not have access to high-quality educational opportunities and fall far short of achieving their academic potential while in school. The Organization for Economic Cooperation and Development (OECD) provides data on comparative student achievement across nations, through its Programme for International Student Assessment (PISA), ranking countries by the reading, science, and math skills of their 15 year-olds. Out of the 29 OECD members for whom test scores were available in 2003, the United

States ranked 15th on reading performance, 19th on science skills, and 24th on math proficiency. These rankings are more dismal when you consider that four of the five countries (Greece, Mexico, Portugal, and Turkey) that ranked lower than the United States on all three measures have per capita GDP's that are less than half that of the United States.[3]

The comparative educational achievement of American children is somewhat better in the fourth and eighth grades according to the Trends in Interational Mathematics and Science Study (TIMSS) of Martin et al. (2004) and Mullis et al. (2004) and to the Progress in International Reading Literacy Study (PIRLS) of Mullis et al. (2003), but, here too, the United States does not rank highly. The TIMSS studies found that, out of a sample of 25 nations, American fourth graders ranked 12th and sixth in math and science proficiency, respectively. American eighth graders ranked 15th out of 46 and 10th out of 48 for math and science achievement, respectively. The PIRLS found that American fourth graders ranked ninth out of 35 countries on reading achievement. Both the TIMSS reports and the PIRLS compare nations that vary greatly in their level of economic development and most of the countries that rank lower than the United States. are much poorer than the United States (such as Egypt, Indonesia, Iran, Morocco, Ghana, and Chile). When the math, science, and reading scores of American children in the TIMSS and PIRLS are compared more appropriately to those of children in other relatively wealthy nations, American children rank roughly in the middle of the pack in fourth and eighth grades.

An earlier TIMSS (Mullis et al. 1998) found that among students in the last year of high school American students ranked near the bottom in math and science: Out of 21 nations, American high school seniors ranked 19th in math and 16th in science. When compared only to seniors in 13 other economically advanced nations, American students ranked second to last in science and dead last in math.

It would be inappropriate to compare this earlier TIMSS to the more recent ones discussed above and conclude that American students are closing the education performance gap with their counterparts in other nations due to the increasing prekindergarten participation rates of American children. The comparisons of seniors are highly problematic given the differences in education systems. For example, many European seniors have 13 years of schooling compared to just 12 years for American seniors. It would also be inappropriate to suggest that the TIMSS studies show slippage in the performance of American students relative to others as they move from fourth to eighth to 12th grade that is attributable to the increasing prekindergarten participation rates of American children. These studies did not follow one cohort of students as they progressed through the educational system, hence they cannot show slippage or improvement over time. Instead, they are each snapshots of the performance of different cohorts of children at one specific moment in time. Furthermore, these studies do not have data on the preschool education enrollment rates of the children they tested. However, it is notable (as observed by Karoly and Bigelow 2005) that most of the countries that score higher than the United States make more substantial investments in preschool education than does the United States.

Poor and non-poor children who fail to achieve their full academic potential are more likely to enter adulthood without the skills necessary to develop into highly productive members of society able to compete effectively in a global labor market. Less skilled, less productive, and earning less, when these children become adults they will be less able to contribute to the growth and development of the U.S. economy.

Not surprisingly then, given the relative poverty and educational underachievement of American children, the skills of American workers do not compare favorably to the skills of workers in other economically advanced nations. The Organization for Economic Cooperation and Development (OECD 2000) has assessed the skills of adults aged 16 to 65 in 20 nations, 13 of which have levels of economic development similar to that of the United States.[4] In terms of the knowledge and skills needed to understand and use information from texts, including editorials, news stories, and instruction manuals (prose literacy), the OECD reports that America ranked 10th out of 14. In terms of the skills and knowledge required to apply arithmetic operations to balance a checkbook, figure out a tip, complete an order form, or determine the amount of interest on a loan from an advertisement (quantitative literacy), American adults ranked 11th out of 14. And, in terms of the knowledge and skills required to use information contained in job applications, payroll forms, transportation schedules, maps, tables, and charts (document literacy), America ranked only 12th out of the 14 economically advanced nations surveyed.

The poverty and the relatively poor educational performance of children and adults explains in part why American workers are not the most productive in the world, even given the stability of our institutions, our advanced technology, the relative abundance of our resources, and our great accumulation of capital goods. According to the OECD, the United States ranked only seventh out of 20 economically advanced nations in labor productivity in 2005 (OECD Productivity Database, January 2006)

The relative shortcomings in productivity and the educational achievement of American children and adults are worrisome as skills are becoming increasingly important for individual, business, and national success in the global economy. An individual's probability of being unemployed decreases as literacy increases: in the United States and elsewhere, individuals with low levels of prose literacy have double the rate of unemployment of those with high levels of literacy (OECD 2000). Similarly, individual earnings rise substantially with literacy proficiency. As a summary of an OECD study put out by the Canadian government points out:[5]

> Individuals are increasingly required not only to have higher levels of education, but also the capacity to adapt, learn, and master changes quickly and efficiently. This requires broad foundation skills that must be regularly updated and complemented with specific skills through training and lifelong learning processes.... Firms require highly skilled employees to compete internationally, to adapt to new technologies and to attain higher levels of efficiency and productivity. Similarly, countries with higher levels of skills will adjust more effectively to challenges and opportunities opened up by globalization.

Or as Knudsen et al. (2006) put it, "The future success of the U.S. economy will depend in part on well-educated and highly resourceful workers who are capable of learning new skills so that they remain competitive in a continually changing global market."

Crime

In the United States, crime rates more than tripled between 1960 and 1980, when they peaked at nearly 6,000 crimes per 100,000 inhabitants. Since 1980, crime rates have fallen substantially to just over 4,000 per 100,000 inhabitants in 2000. Still, about 13 million Americans are victims of crime each year and 1.5 million are victims of violent crime.[6]

The United States does not fare well in international comparisons of crime. The United States (in 2001) has one of the highest prison populations per 100,000 inhabitants of any country in the world: nearly eight times greater than in the 15 European Union (EU) nations, nearly 14 times greater than in Japan, and almost seven times greater than in neighboring Canada. The homicide rate in the United States is nearly three and a half times greater than it is in the EU, five times larger than in Japan, and three times greater than it is in Canada (Barclay and Tavares 2003).

Crime takes an enormous toll on society. The costs of crime come in many forms and include the value of the property stolen from victims; the value of the property damaged by criminals; the medical costs borne by victims; government costs associated with providing police protection, carrying out criminal court processes and running correctional institutions; private security expenditures such as home security systems; and the pain and suffering experienced by victims of rape, assault, child abuse, and other crimes. The total cost of crime is difficult to measure, but researchers have made estimates. For example, the National Institute of Justice (Miller, Cohen, and Wiersema 1996) has estimated that the cost of crimes in the United States committed against persons and households during the period 1987 to 1990 was $450 billion annually.

In short, the United States is failing to achieve its potential in the areas of the well-being of children, the educational achievement and productivity of children and adults, and crime and is falling short relative to other economically advanced nations. But there is hope: economic research is demonstrating that investment in early childhood education is one of the best ways to improve child well-being, increase the educational achievement and productivity of children and adults, and reduce crime. Such investment is also one of the best ways to help us attain numerous other socioeconomic goals. It is interesting to note that the conclusions of economists about the effectiveness of investment in early childhood education are buttressed and strongly supported by the findings of scholars in several other fields of inquiry. Consider the following from Knudsen et al. (2006):

> A cross-disciplinary examination of research in economics, developmental psychology, and neurobiology reveals a striking convergence on a set of common principles that account for the potent effects of early environment on the capacity for human skill development. Central to these principles are the findings that early

> experiences have a uniquely powerful influence on the development of cognitive and social skills, as well as on brain architecture and neurochemistry; that both skill development and brain maturation are hierarchical processes in which higher level functions depend on, and build on, lower level functions; and that the capacity for change in the foundations of human skill development and neural circuitry is highest earlier in life and decreases overtime. These findings lead to the conclusion that the most efficient strategy for strengthening the future workforce, both economically and neurobiologically, and for improving its quality of life is to invest in the environments of disadvantaged children during the early childhood years.

Within the discipline of economics there has long been near universal agreement that educational achievement and attainment are fundamental elements of success in the labor market. Education provides skills, or human capital, that raises an individual's productivity and future earnings.[7] Findings from economics and other fields, such as medicine, neurobiology, and developmental psychology, increasingly indicate that "prevention is more effective and less costly than remediation, and earlier is far better than later" (Knudsen et al. 2006). Thus, there is growing consensus that investment in the education of young children, especially disadvantaged children, is one of the most effective strategies to develop the workforce of the future, improve the quality of life, and enhance the wealth of nations, societies, communities, families, and individuals.

Overview of the benefits of early childhood development programs

Consensus about the effectiveness of investments in high-quality early childhood development (ECD) programs has not always existed. Initially, there was great optimism about the benefits of ECD programs. Early studies showed that children in ECD programs performed significantly better on IQ tests in the first few years after program participation than did comparable children who did not participate in the programs (see, for example, Deutsch 1967). However, follow-up studies of ECD participants found that their advantage over non-ECD participants in terms of IQ test scores and other cognitive educational outcomes tended to fade as they progressed through school so that by the end of third grade there were no significant IQ test score differences (see, for example, a Westinghouse Learning Corporation study by Cicirelli 1969). The initial optimism turned to pessimism and some scholars concluded that investment in ECD was a waste of money, producing few if any lasting benefits but costing thousands of dollars per participant.

Subsequent and better quality research has shown that this pessimism about the longer-term effects of ECD investment is unwarranted for several reasons. First, there was an undue focus on IQ scores at the expense of other cognitive and socio-development outcomes. In general, research has shown that gains in IQ due to ECD program participation are short term and tend to gradually fade and even disappear (Barnett 2004). However, many other important outcomes, such as improvements in achievement test scores and graduation rates, and diminished grade retention, special education placements, and crime and delinquency persist. So, even if gains in IQ fade over time there are numerous other long-term educational and social benefits from ECD program participation.

Second, several studies that found a "fadeout" effect of the educational benefits of ECD participation were methodologically unsound. For example, the famous Westinghouse study mentioned above that continues to be widely cited by non-experts, was seriously flawed for a number of reasons. Below, a few of these flaws are explained.

Children in first, second, and third grade who had attended Head Start were compared to classmates in the same grades who had not attended Head Start. But, children in both groups who were placed in special education were not included in the samples. Since the non-Head Start comparison group had a higher percentage of special education placements, a higher percentage of lower performing children were excluded from the comparison group. In addition, while the two groups of children were appropriately matched on a number of criteria, they were not matched on age. Children retained in grade were included in the samples and mixed in with the younger children in the grade to which they were retained. Again, the non-Head Start comparison group had a higher percentage of children who were retained in grade. Thus, an increasing age gap developed between the comparison group and the Head Start children as they advanced from first to third grade. As a consequence, the third grade comparison group was significantly older than the third grade Head Start group (Barnett and Hustedt 2005). So, what the Westinghouse study found was not fadeout, but that a relatively larger subset of the highest performing Head Start children (those Head Start children not placed in special education) did as well as a relatively smaller subset of the highest performing non-Head Start children (those not placed in special education). In addition, the study found that younger third graders who had attended Head Start performed as well as older third graders who had not attended Head Start, a positive reflection on Head Start given that achievement test scores of children are positively correlated with age. The findings that Head Start participants were less likely to be placed in special education or retained in grade are examples of the lasting educational benefits of prekindergarten that were inappropriately used to suggest the opposite.

Third, studies that report fadeout effects often fail to control for the quality of ECD programs.[8] Numerous studies have found that quality matters: higher quality predicts higher test scores in language and math, fewer behavioral problems, and better work habits *that last over time* (Peisner-Feinberg et al. 2001; Broberg ,Wessel, Lamb, and Hwang 1997; Howes 1988; Vandell, Henderson, and Wilson 1988; NICHD 2005). A recent and large National Institute for Child Health and Development study (NICHD 2005) found that children who experienced better quality child-care manifested greater achievement through the third grade without any fadeout effects. Hence, poor-quality ECD programs may generate small educational benefits that diminish over time, but high-quality programs produce larger benefits that endure.

Thus a strong consensus has developed among experts who have studied high-quality early childhood development programs that these programs have substantial and enduring payoffs. Long-term studies of ECD participants have consistently found that investing in children has several lasting, important benefits for the participants, their families, and society at large including taxpayers. These benefits include:[9]

- Higher levels of verbal, mathematical, and general intellectual achievement
- Greater success at school, including less grade retention, less need for special education, and higher graduation rates
- Higher employment and earnings
- Better health outcomes
- Less welfare dependency
- Lower crime rates
- Higher government revenues and lower government expenditures

More specifically, assessments of well-designed and well-executed programs in early childhood development, several of which are described in detail in the next chapter, have established that participating children are more successful in school and in life after school than children who are not enrolled in high-quality programs. In particular, children who participate in high-quality ECD programs tend to have higher scores on math and reading achievement tests and greater language abilities. They are better prepared to enter elementary school, experience less grade retention, and have less need for special education and other remedial coursework. They have lower dropout rates, higher high school graduation rates, and higher levels of education attainment. They also have better nutrition, improved access to health care services, higher rates of immunization, and better health. Additionally, they experience less child abuse and neglect, and they are less likely to be teenage parents.

As adults, high-quality prekindergarten recipients have higher employment rates, higher earnings, greater self-sufficiency, and lower welfare dependency. They exhibit lower rates of drug use and less frequent and less severe delinquent behavior, engaging in fewer criminal acts both as juveniles and as adults and having fewer interactions with the criminal justice system, and lower incarceration rates. The benefits of ECD programs to participating children enable them to enter school ready to learn, helping them achieve better outcomes in school and throughout their lives.

Parents and families of children who participate in ECD programs also benefit—both directly from the services they receive in high-quality programs and indirectly from the subsidized child care provided by publicly funded ECD programs. For example, mothers have fewer additional births, have better nutrition, and smoke less during pregnancy, and are less likely to abuse or neglect their children. They complete more years of schooling, have higher high school graduation and employment rates, have higher earnings, engage in fewer criminal acts, have lower rates of drug and alcohol abuse, and are less likely to use welfare.

Investments in ECD programs pay for themselves over time by generating very high rates of return for participants, the non-participating public, and government. Good programs produce $3 or more in present value benefits for every dollar of investment. While participants and their families get part of the total benefits, the benefits to the rest of the public and government can be larger and, on their own, tend to far outweigh the costs of these programs. Thus, it is advantageous even for non-participating taxpayers to help pay for these programs.

Several prominent economists and business leaders (many of whom are skeptical about government programs generally) have recently issued well-documented reviews of the literature that find very high economic payoffs from ECD programs. For example, Nobel Prize–winning economist James Heckman of the University of Chicago has concluded:

> Recent studies of early childhood investments have shown remarkable success and indicate that the early years are important for early learning and can be enriched through external channels. Early childhood investments of high-quality have lasting effects....In the long run, significant improvements in the skill levels of American workers, especially workers not attending college, are unlikely without substantial improvements in the arrangements that foster early learning. We cannot afford to postpone investing in children until they become adults, nor can we wait until they reach school age—a time when it may be too late to intervene. Learning is a dynamic process and is most effective when it begins at a young age and continues through adulthood. The role of the family is crucial to the formation of learning skills, and government interventions at an early age that mend the harm done by dysfunctional families have proven to be highly effective (Heckman 1999, 22 and 41).

The director of research and an associate economist at the Federal Reserve Bank of Minneapolis, Arthur Rolnick and Rob Grunewald, have come to similar conclusions:

> ...recent studies suggest that one critical form of education, early childhood development, or ECD, is grossly under-funded. However, if properly funded and managed, investment in ECD yields an extraordinary return, far exceeding the return on most investments, private or public....In the future any proposed economic development list should have early childhood development at the top (Rolnick and Grunewald 2003, 3 and 16).

Likewise, after reviewing the evidence, The Committee for Economic Development (CED), a nonpartisan research and policy organization of some 250 business leaders and educators, concluded that:

> Society pays in many ways for failing to take full advantage of the learning potential of all of its children, from lost economic productivity and tax revenues to higher crime rates to diminished participation in the civic and cultural life of the nation....Over a decade ago, CED urged the nation to view education as an investment, not an expense, and to develop a comprehensive and coordinated strategy of human investment. Such a strategy should redefine education as a process that begins at birth and encompasses all aspects of children's early development, in-

cluding their physical, social, emotional, and cognitive growth. In the intervening years, the evidence has grown even stronger that investments in early education can have long-term benefits for both children and society (Committee for Economic Development 2002).

In its most recent review of the evidence, CED further concluded that:

> ...it has become generally accepted that preschool programs play an important role in preparing children—both advantaged and disadvantaged—to enter kindergarten. There is also a consensus that children from disadvantaged backgrounds in particular should have access to publicly supported preschool programs that provide an opportunity for an "even start."
>
> The social equity arguments for preschool programs have recently been reinforced by compelling economic evidence, which suggests that society at large benefits from investing in these programs. Broadening access to preschool programs for *all* children is a cost-effective investment that pays dividends for years to come and will help ensure our states' and our nation's future economic productivity (Committee for Economic Development 2006).

Reviewing the benefit-cost ratios calculated for three high-quality prekindergarten programs illustrates the net benefits of investment in ECD programs.

Estimates of benefit-cost ratios for prekindergarten investment

Three prekindergarten programs have had carefully controlled studies with long-term follow-up of participants and a control group of non-participants: the Perry Preschool Project, the Abecedarian Early Childhood Intervention, and the Chicago Child-Parent Center Program (CPC).[10] All of these studies, described in more detail in the next chapter, have found that enormous payoffs result from investments in early childhood development. Specifically, as illustrated in **Figure A**, analyses of the three programs for disadvantaged children have found benefit-cost ratios that varied from a minimum of 3.78 to 1 to a high of 17.07 to 1 (expressed in net present value). Investment in a project is justified if its benefits are greater than its costs or if its benefit-cost ratio exceeds 1 to 1.[11] Moreover, in the benefit-cost analyses of all three of these programs, the costs may have been fully described, but the benefits were certainly understated.[12] Thus, the benefits of these prekindergarten programs probably exceed the costs by margins greater than those indicated in Figure A.

From the perspective of public policy, investments in prekindergarten programs pay for themselves by generating very high rates of return for participants, the non-participating public, and government (in the form of either reduced public service costs or higher tax payments by participants and their families). While participants and their families get part of the total benefits, it is noteworthy that the benefits to the non-participating public and government are larger and, in and of themselves, tend to far outweigh

FIGURE A Ratio of benefits to costs

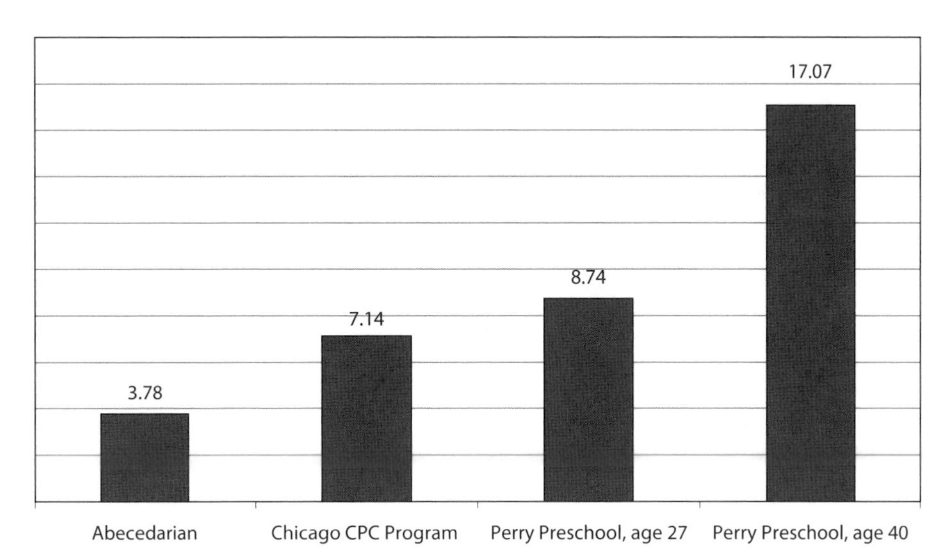

Source: Barnett (1993), Masse and Barnett (2002), Reynolds et al. (2002), and Schweinhart et al. (2005).

the costs of these programs. For example, a Federal Reserve Bank of Minneapolis (Rolnick and Grunewald 2003) study determined that annual real rates of return (i.e., adjusted for inflation) on public investments in the Perry Preschool prekindergarten program were 12% for the non-participating public and government, and 4% for participants, so that total returns exceeded 16%. Thus, it is advantageous even for non-participating taxpayers to pay for these programs. To comprehend how extraordinarily high these rates of return on prekindergarten investments are, consider that the highly touted real rate of return on the stock market that prevailed between 1871 and 1998 was just 6.3% (Burtless 1999).

Even from the narrow perspective of budgetary policy, investments in prekindergarten programs pay for themselves because the costs to government are outweighed by the positive budget impacts that the investments eventually produce. **Figure B** illustrates the benefit-cost ratio for two of the three prekindergarten programs described in Figure A assuming that all the costs are borne by government and taking into account only the benefits that generate budget gains for government.[13] These ratios vary from 2.5 to 1 for the Perry Preschool program to 2.9 to 1 for the Chicago CPC program.

Most earlier research has not translated these calculations of benefits and costs into estimates of how investments in prekindergarten programs affect future government finances, the economy, and crime; this study presents such an analysis based on the outcomes of the Chicago Child-Parent Center program. The next chapter describes in de-

FIGURE B Government benefits for each dollar invested

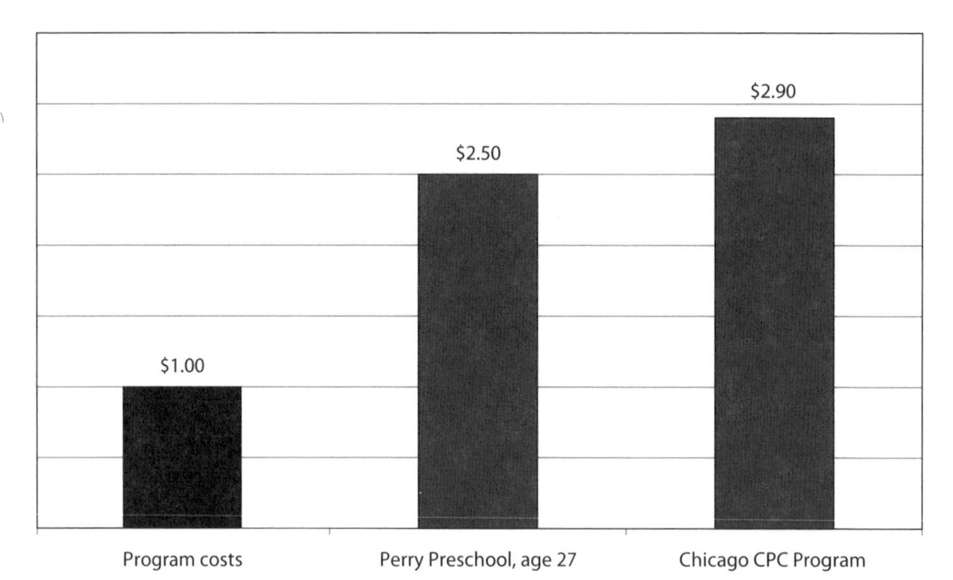

Source: Barnett (1993), Masse and Barnett (2002), Reynolds et al. (2002), and Schweinhart et al. (2005).

tail the long-run effects of the high-quality Perry Preschool, Abecedarian, and Chicago CPC prekindergarten programs and Head Start. The Chicago Child-Parent Center program will be described in particular detail as the outcomes of this program are used as the basis for the analysis carried out in chapters two and three. Chapter two describes the budgetary, economic, and crime effects of a voluntary, high-quality, publicly financed prekindergarten education program targeted *only* to three- and four-year-olds who live in families in the lowest quartile of the income distribution. Chapter three describes the budgetary, economic, and crime effects of a similar, but *universal*, voluntary prekindergarten education program for *all* three- and four-year-old children. In both chapters two and three, the national and state-level effects of prekindergarten are discussed. Appendix A discusses costs and benefits of both prekindergarten programs that may have been omitted from the analyses described in Chapters two and three, and provides a sensitivity analysis that illustrates the range of possible benefits. Appendix B explains the methodology used to carry out the extrapolations in chapters two and three.

CHAPTER 1

The long-run benefits of investments in early childhood development

Evidence from three high-quality prekindergarten programs and Head Start

This chapter begins with a brief description of the general characteristics of early childhood development (ECD) programs. Then, case studies of the benefits of investment in four prekindergarten programs of varying quality are presented: the Perry Preschool Project, the Abecedarian Early Childhood Intervention, Head Start, and the Chicago Child-Parent Center program. The Chicago Child-Parent Center program is described in particular detail—inlcuding the pedagogy and other factors that account for its success—as it is the basis of the cost/benefit estimates described in the following two chapters.

General characteristics of high-quality ECD and prekindergarten programs

In general, high-quality ECD programs target children beginning as early as their prenatal months or as late as four years of age. These programs typically continue assisting participants until the onset of elementary school, but some continue to provide services through the elementary years. Some provide assistance at a center or school, others provide in-home services, and still others combine in-home with center-based care. Services offered typically include language development and core educational services but often include many others such as health services, nutrition education, and social and emotional development services. Some programs are day-long and year round while others are half-day or less and run only part year. High-quality ECD programs do not typically focus exclusively on children: they also provide training and assistance to parents such as parenting instruction, adult education, and employment acquisition education.

Prekindergarten programs are ECD programs that provide services to children ages three and/or four. High-quality prekindergarten education programs have low ratios of children to teachers (10 to 1 or better), small class sizes (20 or lower), and highly paid, well-qualified teachers and staff. Teachers are typically required to have a bachelor's degree with a specialization in early childhood education and assistant teachers are usually required to have at least a child development associate or equivalent degree.

Both teachers and assistants are given opportunities to continue their professional development. In addition, the nature of teacher-child interactions tends to be warm, positive, supportive, and stimulating. Parental involvement is encouraged and cultivated. In good programs, a meal is provided, health services are offered, and safety procedures are carefully followed. The activities in the classroom and the instructional materials vary with emphasis placed on quality instruction in a wide range of fields including art, music, science, math, problem solving, language development, and reasoning. Finally, high-quality prekindergarten programs include monitoring programs and site visits to ensure that quality standards are being implemented.[14]

Head Start is by far the largest of the prekindergarten programs. The other three prekindergarten programs described below were selected because they represent examples of high-quality, well-conceived programs. Perhaps more importantly, these four programs all include long-term follow up studies that analyzed the outcomes of the programs after following the children to the age of 21 (the Abecedarian Early Childhood Intervention), 24 (Chicago Child-Parent Centers), 31 (Head Start), or 40 (Perry Preschool). In addition, these programs took place in a wide variety of settings from small town (Abecedarian and Perry Preschool) to large, urban inner-city (Chicago Child-Parent Centers).

1. Perry Preschool Project *(Ypsilanti, Michigan 1962-1967)*

Description: One hundred twenty-three African American children with low IQs (in the 70 to 85 range) from families with low socio-economic status were randomly assigned to one of two groups: one enrolled in a prekindergarten program and one not. Those enrolled in prekindergarten attended for two school years at ages three and four. Services included daily two-and-a-half-hour classes and weekly one-and-a-half-hour home visits with mother and child. Both groups of children were evaluated annually until they reached the age of 11, and then again at ages 14, 15, 19, 27, and 40.

Results: **Table 3** summarizes some of the statistically significant outcomes of the preschool program. Researchers observed additional positive outcomes from the program, but these benefits are not included in the table or described in the following discussion because it cannot be asserted with a high degree of certainty that they resulted from the ECD investment.

Each time the children were evaluated, important benefits of the prekindergarten program emerged. For example, by age 10 only 17% of the preschool children had been held back a grade or placed in special education compared to 38% of children who had not been placed in prekindergarten. By age 14, the preschoolers had significantly higher achievement scores, and by age 19 they had higher literacy scores and grade-point averages.

The differences in achievement have persisted and in some cases have grown over time. By age 27, 71% of the preschoolers had graduated from high school versus 54% of those not placed in preschool. By age 40, the graduation rate reached 77% for the prekindergarten program group versus 60% for those not in the program. The children

TABLE 3 Statistically significant benefits of the Perry Preschool Project

	Preschoolers	Non-Preschoolers
Grade retention or special education, age 10	17%	38%
High school graduation, age 27	71%	54%
Arrested for drug-related offenses by age 27	9%	25%
Arrested, age 27	48%	57%
Average number of arrests by age 27	2.3	4.6
Earn $2,000 or more per month, age 27	29%	7%
Employment rate, age 27	69%	56%
Average monthly earning, age 27	$1,219	$766
Homeownership, age 40	37%	28%
Car ownership, age 40	82%	60%
Received welfare or social services by age 27	59%	80%
Receiving public assistance, age 27	15%	32%
Single mothers, age 27	57%	83%
Employment, age 40	76%	62%
Median annual earnings, age 27	$12,000	$10,000
Median annual earnings, age 40	$20,800	$15,300
High school graduation, age 40	77%	60%
Earn over $20,000, age 40	60%	40%
Arrested by age 40	71%	83%

Source: (1993), Schweinhart (1993), Karoly et al. (1998 and 2001), and Schweinhart et al. (2005).

in the program had significantly better earnings: at age 27, 29% of preschoolers earned $2,000 or more per month compared to 7% of the non-preschoolers. At age 40, median annual earnings were $20,800 for the program group and $15,300 for the non-program group, or 36% greater, whereas at age 27, the median earnings of the preschoolers were only 20% greater than those of the control group ($12,000 versus $10,000). The employment rate was 69% for the preschoolers at age 27 compared to just 56% for the non-preschoolers and 76% versus 62% at age 40. At age 27, average monthly earnings were 59% higher for the program participants than for non-participants ($1,219 versus $766 in 1993 dollars).

At age 40, 37% of preschoolers owned their own home, and 82% owned a car, whereas only 28% of non-preschoolers owned their own home, and 60% owned a car. At age 27, just 59% of preschoolers had received welfare or other social services in the past 10 years versus 80% of the non-preschoolers. More dramatically, only 15% of preschoolers were receiving public assistance at age 27 compared to 32% of the non-preschoolers. Finally, at age 27, 57% of the female Perry Preschool participants were single mothers compared to 83% of the non-preschoolers.

The effects of the Perry program on crime are substantial. By ages 27 and 40, significantly fewer preschoolers had ever been arrested (48% versus 57% of the control group at age 27 and 71% versus 83% at age 40) and the average number of arrests was about half that of the control group (2.3 lifetime arrests versus 4.6 for the control group at age 27). Nine percent of the preschoolers had been arrested for drug-related offenses compared with 25% of the non-preschoolers.[15]

A benefit-cost analysis by Barnett (1993) found $108,002 in net present value benefits and $12,356 in net present value costs per preschool participant (in 1992 dollars), a benefit-cost ratio of 8.74 to 1. Of the total benefits, the public received $88,433 and $19,570 accrued to the program participants. The benefits to the public included $70,381 saved by potential victims of crimes never committed (based on typical settlements for such crimes) and in reduced justice system costs; $8,846 in higher taxes paid because of higher participants' earnings; $7,155 saved in education costs due primarily to lower grade retention and use of special education; and $2,918 in lower welfare costs. These benefits were partly offset by $868 in increased costs for the public funding of higher education. The benefits to the program participants included $21,485 in higher earnings and fringe benefits and $738 in child care offset by a loss of $2,653 in welfare payments.

Another benefit-cost analysis of the Perry Preschool Project found large net benefits. Karoly et al. (1998) found $49,972 in net present value benefits and $12,148 in net present value program costs in 1996 dollars—a benefit-cost ratio of 4.1 to 1. Karoly et al.'s estimates of benefits differ from those of Barnett mostly because they exclude the benefits that derive from reductions in the intangible losses due to crime: the pain and suffering that crime victims experience. Thus, Barnett calculates $70,381 in benefits from less crime, while Karoly et al. estimate the benefits from less criminal activity at just $20,885. The benefits from reductions in the intangible losses due to crime do not, for the most part, go to government. Thus, while there is a large difference in the overall benefit-cost ratios calculated by Barnett (1993) and Karoly et al. (1998), the benefit-cost ratios they calculate for government savings are very similar: 2.5 to 1 for Barnett and 2.1 to 1 for Karoly et al..

The most recent cost-benefit analysis of the Perry program (Schweinhart et al. 2005), based on the outcomes of participants at age 40, found net present value benefits of $258,888 and net present value costs of $15,166—a benefit-cost ratio of 17.07 to 1. The growth in the benefit-cost ratio over time for the Perry program reflects in part that the benefits of the program persist and even increase as the study participants age.

The economic benefits of the Perry Preschool program were probably underestimated by Barnett (1993), Karoly et al. (1998), and Schweinhart et al. (2005). For example, given that the prekindergarten program was a form of childcare, some of the guardians of program participants were probably able to increase their employment and earnings relative to what they would have been without the program, thus increasing their tax contributions and decreasing their welfare consumption (Karoly et al. 1998). But these benefits were not included in any of the analyses. In addition, none of these analyses calculates the likely positive effects on the children born to participants who have higher earnings and employment and lower incarceration rates (Rolnick and Grunewald 2003). Other savings to government budgets, such as reductions in public health care expenditures, likely resulted from the program, but these benefits were not calculated either.

An analysis of Barnett's (1993) benefit and cost estimate for the Perry Preschool program conducted by the Federal Reserve Bank of Minneapolis estimated the real rate of return for the Perry School program at 16%—12% to society generally, and an additional 4% to the program participants (Rolnick and Grunewald 2003). As the Minneapolis Federal Reserve noted, compared to other public investments and even those in the private sector, such a rate of return on an investment is very high. Indeed, it compares very favorably to the 6.3% real rate of return on the stock market that prevailed between 1871 and 1998 (Burtless 1999).

2. The Abecedarian Early Childhood Intervention
(North Carolina, 1972-85)

Description: One hundred eleven children believed to be at high risk for hindered intellectual and social development based on the low socioeconomic background of their families were enrolled in the program when they were between six and 12 weeks old. The children were randomly assigned to a preschool or a control group. The preschool ran full day, five days a week, and 50 weeks per year. The curriculum stressed language development but attempted to address the social developmental needs of the children, as well. Children in the preschool and in the control group also received medical and nutritional services. At age five all the children were reassigned to either a special school-age intervention program through age eight or to a control group. The intervention program involved having parents engage in specific supplemental education activities for the children in their homes. The parents were given educational material and training roughly every two weeks, with which to engage their children. Data were collected at ages three, five, eight, 12, 15, and 21.

Results: **Table 4** summarizes some of the statistically significant outcomes of the program. Note that these results are from a preschool program that lasted five years from ages zero up to age five. Thus, these results are from the combination of a preschool program for children aged zero to two and a high-quality prekindergarten program for children aged three up to age five. Researchers observed additional positive outcomes from the preschool program, but these benefits have not been included in the table or described in the following discussion because it cannot be asserted with a high degree of certainty that these additional benefits resulted from the ECD investment. The subsequent school-age treatment program from ages five through eight provided some additional benefits, although these effects were weaker than those of the preschool program (see Campbell et al. 2002).

The children who had attended the preschool, whether or not they had participated in the post-age-five intervention program, had significant cognitive achievements relative to the control group children. For example, at ages three, five, eight, 12, and 21 the

TABLE 4 Statistically significant benefits of the Abecedarian Early Childhood Intervention

	Preschool	Control
IQ test, age 21	89.7%	85.2%
Special education, age 9	25.0%	48.0%
Grade retention, age 15	31.0%	55.0%
Years of education, age 21	12.2	11.6
Employed in high skilled jobs, age 21	47.0%	27.0%
Enrolled in four-year colleges, age 21	36.0%	14.0%
Marijuana use in last 30 days, age 21	18.0%	39.0%
Mother additional births	23.0%	40.0%

Source: Masse and Barnett (2002) and Campbell et al. (2002).

preschoolers scored significantly higher on IQ tests than did the control-group children. The preschoolers also scored substantially higher on both math and reading achievement tests at ages eight and 15. By age nine, only 25% of the preschoolers had required special education services compared to 48% of the control-group children. By age 15, only 31% of the preschool participants had ever been retained in grade compared to 55% of those in the control group. By age 21, those who had attended preschool had significantly higher scores on an array of cognitive tests and earned grade equivalent scores in math and reading that were almost two years higher than those of the control group (Campbell et al. 2002). Also by age 21, the preschool attendees had completed significantly more years of education (12.2 years versus 11.6 years) and were more likely to be employed in high-skill jobs (47% versus 27%). Finally, by age 21, 36% of the preschoolers had enrolled in a four-year college versus just 14% of the control group.

In addition to improving measures of intelligence and achievement of the preschoolers, the program had other benefits for the preschoolers as well as benefits for their mothers. For example, at age 21, the preschool participants reported significantly lower rates of marijuana use within the past 30 days (18% versus 39% for the control group) and were less likely to have become a teenage parent (26% versus 45% for the control group). When the preschoolers were approximately four and a half years old, data were collected on the mothers who were under age 18 at the time they gave birth. These young mothers were more likely to have graduated from high school, attained post-high-school education, been employed, and been self-supporting if they were in the intervention group.[16]

Masse and Barnett (2002) conducted a benefit-cost analysis of the Abecedarian Early Childhood Intervention Program in which they calculated $135,546 in benefits and $35,864 in total costs (2002 dollars)—a benefit cost ratio of 3.8 to 1. As was the case for the other benefit-cost analyses discussed above, the benefits were surely underestimated as the researchers limited themselves to benefits for which it was possible to obtain monetary estimates. Thus, Masse and Barnett left out benefits such as the intrinsic value of lower marijuana use, the value of fewer teenage parents, and the value of greater self-sufficiency among the mothers of the preschoolers (Masse and Barnett 2002). In addition, Masse and Barnett did not calculate the government savings in welfare outlays due to the higher earnings of the mothers of participants. Nor did they calculate the added earnings of mothers during the preschool years.

3. Head Start *(1965 to present)*

Description: Head Start is the best-known and largest early childhood intervention program in the United States. It provides early childhood education and development services, health services, and nutrition services to preschool children from low-income families as well as education services for their parents. The program is administered at the local level, with over 1,400 local programs. There is substantial variation in how the program is carried out, but all local programs must comply with federal performance standards and quality guidelines. The typical program runs full-day during one school year for children aged four, but other programs run half-day and accept three-year-olds as well (and two- and five-year-olds in some cases). There are about 900,000 children enrolled annually in the program (less than two-thirds of those who are eligible) at a cost of over $6 billion.

Results: Before discussing the outcomes of the Head Start program, two caveats are in order. First, one should not expect the results of the Head Start program to be as impressive as those of the other programs discussed. While Head Start programs may be of good quality, they are generally ranked lower in quality than the other programs in terms of teacher/pupil ratios, class size, teacher education and experience, and teacher pay. This relatively lower quality is certainly in part due to the fact that the Head Start program is funded at much lower levels than the other programs discussed in this chapter. For example, Karoly et al. (1998) estimated that the Perry Preschool Project costs about $7,000 per child annually (for a half-day program), and estimated that the Abecedarian program costs about $15,000 per child annually (for a full-day program), compared to about $5,000 per child annually (for mostly full-day programs) for the Head Start programs (all amounts expressed in 1996 dollars).

Second, it is difficult to evaluate the overall effectiveness of Head Start. The 1,400 local programs are not uniform (although they must all follow federal guidelines), and there have been no carefully controlled, large scale, long-term randomized studies of the outcomes of the local Head Start programs (although such studies are underway).

Nonetheless, the following outcomes can be reported. In general, most studies have found that the immediate impact of Head Start, whether measured in terms achievement test score or the behavior, motivation, and health outcomes of participating children up to the start of elementary school, has been small but positive. In terms of IQ test scores, the results of Head Start programs have been found to be quite variable. Specifically, some studies found that Head Start had no effect on IQ test scores, many found positive initial effects that faded by ages seven through 11, and a few studies found longer-term positive effects on test scores.

Long-term studies of Head Start suggest that some of the positive and immediate cognitive effects, although they may not fade out altogether, do diminish over time. But other effects such as reductions in grade retention and special education persist over time.

Currie and Thomas (2000) found that the fading of Head Start gains may be due to the fact that Head Start students, particularly non-white children, are more likely to attend inferior schools subsequent to the Head Start program than are non-Head Start children. Indeed, white Head Start students who attend schools of similar quality to other white students maintain the initial gains in test scores. This suggests that in order to prevent the fade out of the gains of Head Start, the quality of subsequent schooling must be improved. And, of course, the fact that the Head Start children are more likely to attend inferior schools subsequent to the Head Start program than are non-Head Start children may make comparisons between the groups inappropriate. If we want to understand the effects of Head Start versus non-Head Start (including any fade out effect), then we should compare students who have subsequent access to schools of similar quality.

Barnett (2002) argues that the fade out of Head Start-induced achievement test score gains found in some studies may not be occurring at all. He points out that Head Start students' achievement test scores have been improperly compared to non-Head Start students' scores because of high attrition in the samples and other methodological design flaws. The flaws discussed earlier with respect to the Westinghouse Study (1969) of Head Start—where the scores of children held back or placed in special education were not properly included in the samples—are a prime example of this problem. Barnett notes that studies that do not have these design flaws have been more likely to find persistent positive effects of Head Start on achievement test scores.

Only one Head Start study (of the program in Rome, Georgia) followed the children through high school. It found that Head Start had a large positive effect on high school graduation rates. Head Start participation was also associated with higher immunization rates.

There is some evidence of the long-term benefits of Head Start. A comparison (Garces et al. 2000) of Head Start participants to non-participants between the ages of 18 and 31 found that white and Latino participants had a significantly higher probability of completing high school and attending college. In addition, white participants had elevated earnings in their early 20s. For white children whose mothers had less than a high school education, attending Head Start led to a 28% increase in high school graduation, a 27% increase in attending college, and a 100% increase in earnings in their early 20s. African American participants had a significantly lower probability of ever being charged or convicted of a crime, and African American male participants were more likely than their siblings to have completed high school.

Oden, Schweinhart, and Weikart (2000) also found some evidence of the long-term benefits of Head Start. They analyzed 622 22-year-olds, 17 years after their participation or non-participation as children in Head Start programs at two sites (one in Florida and one in Colorado). In the samples from Florida, 95% of the female Head Start participants had obtained a high school diploma or General Education Development (GED) diploma compared to just 81% of the female non-participants. In addition, only 5% of the female Head Start participants had ever been arrested compared to 15% of the female non-participants. They further found that the children who had attended Head Start classes using an enhanced curriculum rather than the standard Head Start curriculum had significantly higher grades throughout their schooling and less than half as many criminal convictions by age 22 as the non-participants.

Ludwig and Miller (2005) found that Head Start had a large impact on the mortality rates of children aged five through nine as well as positive effects on educational attainment. They suggest that a 50% to 100% increase in Head Start funding for their high-poverty treatment group could reduce the child mortality rates of this group by 33% to 75%. They also found that children exposed to Head Start, regardless of race, had statistically significant improvements in high school completion and college attendance.

As mentioned above, it would be unreasonable to expect Head Start to generate the same positive results as the other model ECD programs, in part because the Head Start programs are funded at much lower levels per student than are the other programs. Currie and Neidell (2003) provide strong evidence that funding levels matter. They found that Head Start children in higher per student spending programs have significantly larger gains on reading scores and a lower probability of grade retention than do Head Start children in lower spending programs.

Finally, the National Head Start Impact Study has recently published its first year findings (Puma et al. 2005) from a study that plans to follow children for four years. Approximately 5,000 three- and four-year-old children were randomly assigned to Head Start or a non-Head Start group (whose members could enroll in programs other than Head Start). After one year of Head Start, there were small to moderate statistically significant positive impacts for both three- and four-year-olds on several measures of cognitive achievement. In addition, there were small statistically significant impacts on social emotional behavior for three-year-olds but not for four-year-olds. In terms of access to health care and health status there were small to moderate improvements for three-year-olds. For four-year-olds, there were moderately positive impacts on access to health care but significant impacts on their health status. Lastly, there were small statistically significant improvements in the parenting practices of parents of both three and four-year-olds who had attended Head Start.

Again, it should be noted that it would be unreasonable to expect the same outcomes from Head Start that are observed in the high-quality prekindergarten programs described here. As Barnett and Hustedt (2005) argue, "...it seems highly plausible that programs such as Head Start lack the type of funding necessary to produce the levels of intensity and quality achieved in better funded model programs with the direct result that they are less effective."

4. The Chicago Child-Parent Center program

(Chicago, Illinois, 1967 to present)

Description: Established in 1967, the Child-Parent Center Program (CPC) provides center-based, comprehensive educational and family-support services to economically disadvantaged children from prekindergarten (ages three or four) to early elementary school (up to grade three/age nine). The program was initiated with funding from Title I of the Elementary and Secondary Education Act of 1965, and its prekindergarten and kindergarten components are still supported by those federal funds. After Head Start, CPC is the oldest federally funded prekindergarten program in the nation and the oldest extended early-childhood program.

To be eligible for enrollment in the CPC, children must live in school neighborhoods that receive Title I funding. In contrast to Head Start, neighborhood poverty, rather than individual poverty, is the first criterion for program eligibility, though both practices result in an intake of a high proportion of children living in poverty. However, CPC prekindergarten programs exist only in some of the neighborhoods that receive Title I funding. To encourage the enrollment of high-need youngsters in the neighborhoods where the programs exist, school-community representatives who work in the centers conduct a variety of outreach activities, even going door-to-door. Eligible children must not be enrolled in another preschool program, and their parents must agree to participate in the program at least one-half day per week in classroom activities, field trips, or adult education classes; in practice, participation tends to be lower.

The CPC programs are conducted under the auspices of the Chicago Public School system, operating either in a separate building in close proximity to the local elementary school or in a wing of the elementary school. A head teacher directs each center and coordinates the child education program, parent involvement, community outreach, health, and nutrition services. The centers have their own budgets and administrative operations, but each head teacher reports directly to the principal of the associated elementary school.

Teachers in the CPC program have at least a bachelor's degree, with certification in early childhood education (Graue et al. 2004, 8). This is in sharp contrast to Head Start and many other preschool programs, which, unlike the public school system, can hire "teachers" without a minimum of a four-year college degree. Relative to Head Start and most preschool programs, staff stability and compensation are high (i.e., the salary schedule of the public schools), with the latter strongly contributing to the former (Masse and Barnett 2002).

Aside from qualified teachers, individual classrooms are staffed by teacher aides (one per classroom) and, often, parent volunteers. Centers also have the services of a clerk and a janitor, as well as nurses (who provide health screenings), speech therapists, and other staff from their associated elementary schools. Each center includes a parent-resource teacher who implements the parent program in the parent resource room, with the input of the participants. In addition to conducting outreach activities in the neighborhoods, the school-community representatives associated with each center also make home visits. The Chicago CPC program also provides funds and time for the ongoing professional development of head teachers, classroom teachers and aides, the parent-resource teachers, and the school-community representatives.

Children typically enter the program at age three for a half-day of prekindergarten (morning or afternoon sessions of three hours). Kindergarten is offered at most sites and is either half-day or full-day. The school year follows the regular nine-month school calendar. Beginning in 1977, an elementary school component (grades one through three) was added to the CPC program.[17]

In the prekindergarten program, maximum class size is 17. With a teacher and aide for each classroom, the child/staff ratio is no more than 17 to 2. In the kindergarten program, maximum class size is 25. With a teacher and aide for each classroom, the child/staff ratio is no greater than 25 to 2. In both prekindergarten and kindergarten, parent volunteers further lower the child/staff ratios.

According to information last updated in January 2006, 1,383 children in 48 classrooms across 15 schools/locations were enrolled in the CPC prekindergarten program in 2005.[18] At its height, the CPC prekindergarten program operated in 24 schools/locations. Nineteen of these centers also provided half-day or full-day kindergartens and 13 of the centers provided additional educational services through the third grade when children typically reach nine years of age. Between the prekindergarten programs, the kindergartens, and the elementary school component, over 5,000 children annually are attending the centers.

The centers emphasize basic language and reading skills as well as social and psychological development. The centers also provide free breakfasts, lunches, and health services.

The Chicago Longitudinal Study (1999) has been following a sample of 1,539 children born in 1980 from families of low socioeconomic status. All 989 children who completed the Chicago CPC prekindergarten program and kindergarten were compared to a control group of 550 children who did not attend the preschool program but had participated in full-day kindergarten. Of the 550 children in the control group, 161 attended a CPC kindergarten program even though they had not attended the CPC prekindergarten program. Data on both the intervention and control groups are collected periodically, with the most recent published results having analyzed data for over 20 years, or until the students were 24 years old (Reynolds et al. 2006).

Results: **Table 5** summarizes some of the statistically significant outcomes of the CPC preschool program as reported by Reynolds et al. (2002). The results shown here are only for the education program that served three- and four-year old children in the prekindergarten program. Numerous other statistically significant outcomes have been observed along with positive impacts that were not statistically significant. In addition, other benefits were observed for children who attended the program from preschool through the third grade. In other words, there are good results from the prekindergarten program alone and outcomes continue to improve with later intervention. Many of these other outcomes have been reported in Reynolds et al. (2002) and Reynolds et al. (2006).

TABLE 5 Statistically significant benefits of the Chicago-Parent Center Prekindergarten Program

	Center students	Non-center students
Special education by age 18	14.4%	24.6%
Grade retention, age 15	23.0%	38.4%
Years in special education, from ages 6-18	0.73	1.43
Arrested by age 18	16.90%	25.1%
Arrests for violent offenses by age 18	9.0	15.3
High school graduation, age 20	49.7%	38.5%
Highest grade completed, age 20	10.55	10.23
Victim of abuse or neglect, ages 4-17	5.0%	10.3%
Petitions to juvenile court	0.45	0.78

Source: Reynolds et al. (2002).

The Chicago Longitudinal Study (CLS) has demonstrated that numerous benefits have been generated by the centers. For example, the study found that the center children had significantly higher achievement test scores at ages five, six, nine, and 14 than non-center students. Center students also spent less time in special education through age 18 (0.7 years versus 1.4 years) and had lower grade retention at ages nine and 15 (19% and 23% versus 26% and 38%, repectively). Between the ages of four and 17, 5% of the prekindergarten attending children had been victims of abuse or neglect compared to 10% of the comparison group. Delinquency rates were significantly lower for the center children through ages 13 and 14. By age 18 only 17% of center prekindergarten children had been arrested compared to 25% of the non-center children, charges for violent offenses were brought against 9% of center children but 15% of non-center children, and the number of petitions to juvenile court were 0.45 for the prekindergarten children versus 0.78 for the non-program children. By age 20, the high school graduation rate for center children was 50% compared to just 39% for non-center children.

Reynolds et al. (2002) carried out a benefit-cost analysis of the Chicago Child-Parent Center program. For the prekindergarten program alone, they identified $47,759 in net present value benefits and $6,692 in net present value costs in 1998 dollars—a benefit-cost ratio of 7.1 to1. The benefits derived mainly from reduced public education expenditures due to lower grade retention and use of special education, reduced costs to the criminal justice system and victims of crime due to lower crime rates, higher projected earnings of center participants, and increased income tax revenue due to projected higher lifetime earnings of center participants. When the benefits from reduced pain and suffering on the part of crime victims were included, the benefit-cost ratio for the Chicago CPC prekindergarten program rose to 10.15 to 1.

Once again, the benefits of the program were underestimated. For example, the savings from reduced adult welfare usage on the part of center participants was not calculated. In addition, the likely gains from improved health, changes in fertility behavior, and other life changes were not monetized. Moreover, the likely benefits to offspring of center participants were not calculated nor was the value of the likely increase in parental earnings, due to the child care provided by the preschool, included.

Chicago Child-Parent Center program: What makes it work?

Arthur J. Reynolds and his associates, who, to date, have conducted the most comprehensive longitudinal evaluation of the CPC, deemed seven major features as "critical to the total success of the program." In their words, they are:

1. A structured and diverse set of language-based instructional activities designed to promote academic and social success.
2. Low child-to-teacher ratios in preschool (17 to 2) and kindergarten (25 to 2) in order to provide more intensive and individualized learning.
3. A multi-faceted parent program that includes participating in parent room activities, volunteering in the classroom, attending school events, and enrolling in educational courses for personal development, all under the supervision of the parent-resource teacher.
4. Outreach activities coordinated by the school-community representative, including resource mobilization, home visitation, and enrollment of children most in need.
5. On-going staff development for all center personnel.
6. Health and nutrition services, including health screening, speech therapy, shared nursing services, and free breakfasts and lunches.
7. A comprehensive school-age program from first to third grade that supports children's transition to elementary schools through (a.) reduced class sizes (to 25 children), (b.) the addition of teacher aides in each class, (c.) extra instructional supplies, and (d.) coordination of instructional activities, staff development, and parent-program activities by the free-standing curriculum-parent resource teacher.[19]

A more detailed description of several of the Chicago CPC's critical success factors follows. Because the most recent research on the CPC "indicates that the successful integration of a diverse set of classroom learning activities and opportunities for parent involvement are the origins of the long-term effects of preschool participation in the Child-Parent centers reported in previous studies...and possibly in other programs for children at risk," the following section pays particular attention to curriculum and pedagogy/instructional approaches and parent involvement (Gruae et al. 2004, 26).

Curriculum

Prekindergarten: As Reynolds notes, "the philosophy of the Child-Parent Centers has consistently emphasized the acquisition of basic knowledge and skills in language arts and math through a relatively structured but diverse set of learning experiences (e.g., whole class, small groups, individualized activities, and field trips). While not ignoring the importance of psychological development and self-confidence, these affective learning outcomes were built into the reading and language-based instructional activities....The foundational skills of recognizing letters and numbers, oral communication, listening, and an appreciation for reading and drawing were of primary importance" (Reynolds 2000, 36).

This is not to say, however, that CPC uses a highly scripted, standardized, "academic" or teacher-directed curriculum approach. Instead, the CPC curriculum can best be described "as an amalgam of standardization and local control, academic and social-emotional development" (Graue et al. 2004, 9). On the one hand, teachers have latitude in selecting instructional materials for their classrooms to adapt to classroom needs. On the other hand, beginning in the early 1980s, the district encouraged them to supplement their instructional materials with a standardized curricular approach such as the Chicago Early Assessment and Remediation Laboratory program, or EARLY, which was developed by the Board of Education's Department of Research and Evaluation (Reynolds 2000).

Kindergarten: According to Reynolds' 2000 account of the kindergarten component of the CPC program, classrooms mostly followed the Comprehensive Reading Program (CRP), which was in use throughout the school district. CRP is a mastery learning approach to instruction, designed to promote the development of basic skills in language arts and math.

As they had in prekindergarten, children pursued reading and writing through a diverse array of experiences in and outside the classroom. Reynolds notes that field trips were especially significant and were frequent both in preschool and in kindergarten, with parent volunteers almost always accompanying the class. He cites the Museum of Science and Industry, the Lincoln Park or Brookfield Zoos, public libraries, the Art Institute, the railroad depot, and local businesses as examples of places visited. "Upon return, events and observations from the trip served as a basis for classroom and small group discussion" (Reynolds 2000, 39-40).[20]

Elementary school (grades one through three in the six original CPC schools, grades one and two in the others, due to lack of funding): At the elementary level, curricular distinctions between the Chicago CPC and the rest of the school system diminish. However, because Chicago CPC classrooms have fewer students, more adults, a wider array of instructional supplies and materials, and an ongoing parent program, CPC participants experienced "a more intensive, individualized education than their comparison-group counterparts" (Reynolds 2000, 44-5).

Pedagogy/instructional approach[21]

Some of the best information about the pedagogical/instructional approaches of the CPC prekindergarten and kindergarten teachers comes from two analyses of a 1995 retrospective survey of head teachers who had worked in the program for the years 1983-86. The survey was designed to elicit the extent to which Centers represented a teacher-directed or child-initiated/developmental approach, which, much like the reading "wars" over phonics versus whole language, is a hotly contested pedagogical issue.

In 2000, Reynolds classified the classroom activities at the 20 centers in his study as either teacher oriented or initiated, or developmental/child oriented, or roughly equal in their approaches. Teacher oriented was defined as emphasizing "large-group activities, academic skills, and a structured set of instruction materials (e.g., workbooks, basal readers). Prereading instruction was more frequent as well." Developmental was defined as emphasizing "child-initiated activities in small-group settings, interest centers, and the use of materials such as the Peabody Language Kits and Bank Street Readers as well as the EARLY. Less emphasis was devoted to prereading activities and more to social development" (Reynolds 2000, 40).

Noting that all centers used diverse instructional approaches and therefore fell in the middle range of a "continuum from teacher-oriented to developmental activities," Reynolds reported that seven of the 20 centers were classified as primarily teacher oriented, 10 as developmental, and three as mixed. These classifications are most pertinent to the preschool component of CPC because in kindergarten, "most of the centers were relatively structured and oriented toward the development of academic skills."[22]

In 2004, Graue et al. (including Reynolds), again using the 1995 survey, extended this analysis to assign the 989 children who attended prekindergarten in these 20 Centers in 1983-85 and kindergarten in 1985-86 into one of four instructional groups: high teacher-directed instruction and high child-initiated instruction; high teacher-directed instruction and low child-initiated instruction; low teacher-directed instruction and high child-initiated instruction; and low teacher-directed instruction and low child-initiated instruction. Overall, the researchers found that "76% of CPC children attended centers rated high in child-initiated activities (e.g., learning centers, small group activities), and 46% attended centers rated high in teacher-directed activities (e.g., large-group activities, basic skills emphasis), which was measured independently of child-initiated instruction. Among the four curriculum groups, the largest percentage of children (39.1%) attended centers emphasizing high levels of teacher-directed and child-initiated instructional strategies. Thirty-seven percent of children were in centers characterized as high in child-initiated activities and low in teacher-directed activities. The smallest percentages of children were in centers with relatively low teacher-directed and low child-initiated activities (18%) and with high teacher directed but low child-initiated activities (6%)" (Graue et al. 2004, 15). They concluded that their findings indicated that instructional approaches that blended a teacher-directed focus with child-initiated activities and parental school involvement are most consistently associated with the positive long-term effects of participation in the Child-Parent Centers (Graue et al. 2004, 1-2).

Because parent involvement in school activities was independently associated with child outcomes from kindergarten readiness to eighth grade reading achievement and grade retention, above and beyond curriculum/pedagogical approaches, the parent component of CPC is considered next.

Parent involvement

A central principle of the Chicago CPC program is that "parent involvement is the critical socializing force in children's development. Direct parent involvement in the program is expected to enhance parent-child interactions, parent and child attachment to school, and social support among parents, and consequently to promote children's school readiness and social adjustment" (Reynolds 2000, 41).[23]

The Chicago CPC requires, in theory, parents to participate in the preschool program at least one-half day per week; in practice, participation is less. Each CPC site has a parent room, located adjacent to the classrooms, and its programming is organized by a full-time parent-resource teacher, who has a budget for that purpose.

The parent-resource teacher "organizes the parent room in order to implement parent educational activities, initiate interactions among parents, and foster parent-child interactions. Areas of parent training include consumer education, nutrition, personal development, health and safety, and homemaking arts. Parents may also attend GED classes at the centers. Through their service on the School Advisory Council, parents assist staff in planning and implementation" (Reynolds 2000, 41-2).

A wide range of parent activities is encouraged, "including parent-room activities (e.g., arts and crafts projects), classroom volunteering, participating in school activities, taking part in class field trips, helping to prepare breakfasts and lunches, and engaging in education and training activities" (Reynolds 2000, 42).

The Chicago Longitudinal Study research team has published a number of studies on the impact of parent involvement on child outcomes for CPC.[24] In general, the results of these studies suggest that parental involvement in early education programs significantly and positively influence children's outcomes (Graue et al. 2004).

In short, the keys to the success of the Chicago CPC preschool program include its structured but flexible language-based curriculum, its blend of teacher-directed and child-initiated learning activities, and its extensive parental involvement. Other factors that help account for the more significant and enduring effects of the Chicago CPC program relative to most other early childhood education programs include its small classes and child/teacher ratios, its combination of health and nutrition services, its support and high pay for well-educated staff, and its provision of up to six years of services for children, from ages three to nine, which creates a school-stable environment during preschool and the early primary-grade years (Reynolds 2000, 35).

In the next two chapters, we use the outcomes of the Chicago CPC program to estimate the long-run costs and benefits of voluntary, high-quality, publicly funded prekindergarten. Chapter two describes the results for a voluntary prekindergarten program targeted at relatively poor three- and four-year-old children and chapter three describes the outcomes for a voluntary universal prekindergarten program made available to *all* three- and four-year-old children.

CHAPTER 2

The effects of a voluntary, high-quality, publicly funded, targeted prekindergarten education program on future government finances, the economy, and crime

We begin our benefit-cost analysis by examining a targeted prekindergarten education program, made available only to children below a certain household income threshold. To estimate the long-run costs and benefits of a targeted preschool education program, we must make assumptions about the characteristics of the program. This study assumes a voluntary, high-quality, publicly funded prekindergarten program that is modeled on the Chicago Child-Parent Center program, which was described in detail in chapter one. The program would operate three hours per day, five days a week, for 35 weeks a year (the school year) or a total of 525 hours.[25] The targeted program would be voluntary, and available to all three- and four-year-old children who live in families with incomes of up to 125% of the family poverty level.[26] This income would place them in roughly the bottom quartile of the income distribution. The lead classroom teachers would all have bachelor's degrees (or higher) with certification in early childhood education, and would be required to pursue professional development. The teaching assistant in each class would have at least an associate's degree. Teacher and staff pay would be high relative to most existing preschool programs, as compensation would follow the salary schedules of the public schools. The prekindergarten program would provide health screenings, speech therapy services, and home visitations. Parental involvement would be encouraged. The student/teacher ratio (including the assistant teacher) would be no higher than 17 to 2 and maximum class size would be 17 children. The curriculum would be comprehensive with a focus that includes language and pre-reading skills, mathematic skills such as counting and number recognition, science, social studies, health and physical development, and social/emotional skill development.

We assume that the targeted prekindergarten education program would be largely housed within the existing or newly built public school infrastructure, but its services could be delivered in private care centers as well, if they met quality standards. All costs of the prekindergarten program would be paid for with public monies.

The research literature reviewed in chapter one establishes that high-quality prekindergarten education programs can generate significant long-run benefits for program participants, their families, and other non-participants. This section translates the measured impacts of the Chicago CPC program into estimates of how public investment in a targeted, high-quality prekindergarten program would affect future government finances, the economy, and crime. The methodology used to arrive at the estimates presented below is explained in detail in Appendix B.

Total benefits

The annual budgetary, earnings, and crime benefits of a voluntary, high-quality, publicly funded, targeted prekindergarten program would begin to exceed the annual costs of the program within six years and would do so by a growing margin every year thereafter. By the year 2050, the annual benefits would total $315 billion ($83 billion in government budget benefits, $156 billion in increased compensation of workers, and $77 billion in reduced costs to individuals from less crime and child abuse) and would surpass the costs of the program in that year by a ratio of 12.1 to 1.[27] Broken down by state, in 2050 the total annual benefits would outstrip the annual costs of the program by a minimum of 8.1 to 1 for residents of Alabama and by as much as 29.1 to 1 for the residents of Delaware (see **Table 6**). The annual budgetary, earnings, and crime benefits are further detailed below.

Budget effects

Follow-up research on children who participated in high-quality prekindergarten programs and control groups of similar but non-participating children has found that prekindergarten investments benefit taxpayers in at least four ways. First, subsequent public K-12 education expenses are lower because participants fail fewer grades and require special education less often. Second, criminal justice system costs drop because participants, both as juveniles and as adults, have markedly lower crime and delinquency rates. Third, pre-K investment reduces public child-welfare expenditures because participants and their families are involved in many fewer cases of child abuse and neglect. Fourth, both participants and their parents have higher incomes and thus pay more taxes than non-participants. Against these four types of budget benefits, we must consider three types of budget costs: the expenses of the pre-K program itself, increased expenditure on public high school (participants spend more time in high school), and the increased expenditure on public higher education due to greater colleges and university attendance by pre-K participants.

High-quality prekindergarten programs do not perform miracles on children. As chapter one shows in detail, substantial numbers of pre-K participants do poorly in school, commit crimes, have poor health outcomes, and require government support. The key point is that pre-K participants *as a group* have far lower rates of these negative outcomes than do non-participants.

TABLE 6 (Part 1 of 2) State-by-state costs and benefits of targeted program in 2050

	Government budget benefits (millions of 2006 dollars)	Increased compensation (millions of 2006 dollars)	Savings to individuals from reduced crime (millions of 2006 dollars)	Total budget, compensation, and crime benefits (millions of 2006 dollars)	Ratio of total annual benefits to program costs
National	$82,659	$155,519	$76,969	$315,147	12.1
Alabama	890	2,219	594	3,703	8.1
Alaska	197	452	217	865	13.1
Arizona	2,681	4,917	3,217	10,814	11.4
Arkansas	822	1,393	722	2,937	12.0
California	12,551	25,670	9,750	47,971	12.1
Colorado	1,052	2,090	1,455	4,596	16.7
Connecticut	667	1,347	489	2,504	23.8
Delaware	111	211	123	445	29.1
District of Columbia	387	656	367	1,410	10.3
Florida	5,897	8,995	5,580	20,472	9.9
Georgia	3,376	6,019	3,122	12,517	11.3
Hawaii	217	458	245	920	17.3
Idaho	395	763	573	1,731	13.1
Illinois	3,134	6,185	2,914	12,233	12.6
Indiana	1,327	2,982	1,549	5,858	9.8
Iowa	526	1,096	550	2,172	13.1
Kansas	654	1,230	618	2,502	14.1
Kentucky	1,205	1,961	1,220	4,386	17.5
Louisiana	1,086	2,058	1,248	4,392	11.9
Maine	177	347	190	714	16.2
Maryland	1,243	2,511	1,065	4,820	13.6
Massachusetts	874	1,998	537	3,409	13.6
Michigan	2,414	4,702	1,385	8,501	13.8
Minnesota	982	1,829	1,139	3,950	27.0
Mississippi	796	1,574	1,004	3,374	12.3
Missouri	1,283	2,580	1,124	4,987	12.6

TABLE 6 (Part 2 of 2) State-by-state costs and benefits of targeted program in 2050

	Government budget benefits (millions of 2006 dollars)	Increased compensation (millions of 2006 dollars)	Savings to individuals from reduced crime (millions of 2006 dollars)	Total budget, compensation, and crime benefits (millions of 2006 dollars)	Ratio of total annual benefits to program costs
Montana	$177	$328	$210	$716	13.2
Nebraska	359	719	413	1,491	13.9
Nevada	805	1,535	1,095	3,436	11.0
New Hampshire	149	352	124	626	15.2
New Jersey	1,175	2,520	896	4,591	16.3
New Mexico	549	1,019	599	2,168	12.1
New York	5,942	8,884	4,533	19,359	12.0
North Carolina	2,762	4,941	2,548	10,251	8.8
North Dakota	91	164	130	386	24.1
Ohio	2,477	4,652	2,442	9,571	16.7
Oklahoma	658	1,471	772	2,901	13.3
Oregon	949	1,826	1,202	3,978	15.3
Pennsylvania	2,634	4,740	2,530	9,903	12.4
Rhode Island	249	479	202	929	11.6
South Carolina	1,081	2,025	943	4,049	9.8
South Dakota	179	344	192	715	14.2
Tennessee	1,550	2,952	991	5,492	9.2
Texas	8,962	18,966	9,899	37,828	11.3
Utah	687	1,480	916	3,083	13.7
Vermont	77	154.4	34	266	20.4
Virginia	1,428	3,516	883	5,826	10.5
Washington	1,607	3,342	1,408	6,357	12.8
West Virginia	289	563	142	994	11.8
Wisconsin	1,385	2,559	1,161	5,104	13.6
Wyoming	83	154	125	362	19.7

Source: Author's analysis.

We examine the budget effects through the year 2050 of launching a permanent, high-quality prekindergarten program in 2007 that targets the poorest three- and four-year-old children in America, those who reside in families in the bottom quarter of the income scale. For illustration purposes, we assume that the program would be fully phased in by 2008. We consider budget effects on all levels of government: federal, and state and local combined. We also examine the budget effects on a state-by-state basis. Although responsibilities have shifted in the last half-century and will continue to do so over the nearly half-century time frame used in this study, we assume that all levels of government will share in the costs of education, criminal justice, and child welfare in the future in the same proportions as they do in the present. Likewise, we assume that federal, state, and local tax rates will remain constant over the period analyzed in this study. All the costs and benefits are expressed in (real or inflation-adjusted) 2006 dollars.

A high-quality targeted prekindergarten program would cost nearly $6,300 per participant and could be expected to enroll just over 2 million children in 2008 when it is fully phased in. Thus, the program would cost taxpayers $13.2 billion in 2008. However, some of this money is already being spent on related programs. For example, 38 states have publicly financed prekindergarten programs for some three- and four-year-old children, some of whom would be enrolled in our proposed program. Similarly, all states and the federal government pay for special education and Head Start services for young children, some of whom would attend our proposed program. Hence, some of the current expenditures on state prekindergarten programs and some of the current expenditures on special education and Head Start services are for children who will be attending the proposed targeted prekindergarten program. We assume that these current expenditures would be used to pay for part of the costs of the proposed pre-K program. The bottom line is that our proposed high-quality prekindergarten program would require approximately $8.2 billion in *additional* government outlays in 2008 once it is fully phased in.

Initially, the costs of the program will be relatively stable, growing over time only with inflation and increases in the child population served. These costs will reflect only the actual expenditures on the pre-K program. Eventually, however, there will be additional increases in government expenditures due to the increased educational attainment of pre-K participants. Increased public high school costs first appear when the first cohort of participants turns 17, and increased higher education costs first appear when the first cohort turns 18.

On the other hand, there will be offsetting budget benefits. They will be small initially, but they will grow rapidly over time and eventually outstrip the costs. Budget savings in the first year of the program manifest themselves as reductions in child welfare expenditures as fewer children will be the victims of child abuse and neglect. In addition, some parents take advantage of the fact that part of their child-care needs will be covered by the prekindergarten program. They enter the labor force, secure employment, and pay more in taxes. When the pre-K participants enter the K-12 public school system, additional budget savings begin to appear, as these children will be less likely to repeat a grade or need expensive special education services. When the first cohort

FIGURE C Total budget costs and benefits of targeted program

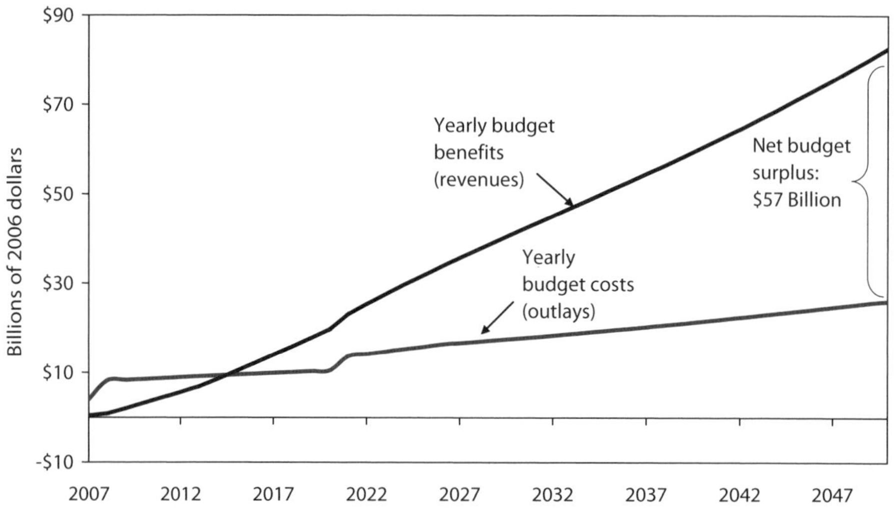

Source: Author's analysis.

of children turns 10 further budget savings will begin to be realized as lower juvenile crime rates require less expenditure on the juvenile justice system. The pre-K participants, as adults, will be less engaged in crime, have higher educational attainment, and earn more income that will eventually generate savings to the adult criminal justice system and increase tax revenue derived from their labor earnings.

Offsetting budget benefits take a while to outstrip the costs, but once they do, the gap becomes substantially favorable over time. For the first eight years of a national program, costs exceed offsetting budget benefits, but by a declining margin. Thereafter, starting in 2015, offsetting budget benefits exceed costs by a growing margin each year. This pattern is illustrated in **Figures C** and **D**. Annual revenue costs and benfits are portrayed in real (inflation-adjusted) terms in Figure C. Figure D shows the annual net budget impact in real terms.

In the second year of the program, 2008, when the program is fully phased in, government outlays exceed offsetting budget benefits by $7.3 billion. The annual pre-kindergarten program related deficit shrinks for the next six years. By the ninth year of the program, 2015, the deficit turns into a surplus that grows every year thereafter culminating in a net budgetary surplus of some $57 billion (in 2006 dollars) in 2050, the last year estimated, as illustrated in Figure C. Thus by 2050, every dollar spent on the program by taxpayers is offset by $3.18 in budget savings (**Table 7**), or $83 billion, in that year.

FIGURE D Net benefits to government budgets from targeted program

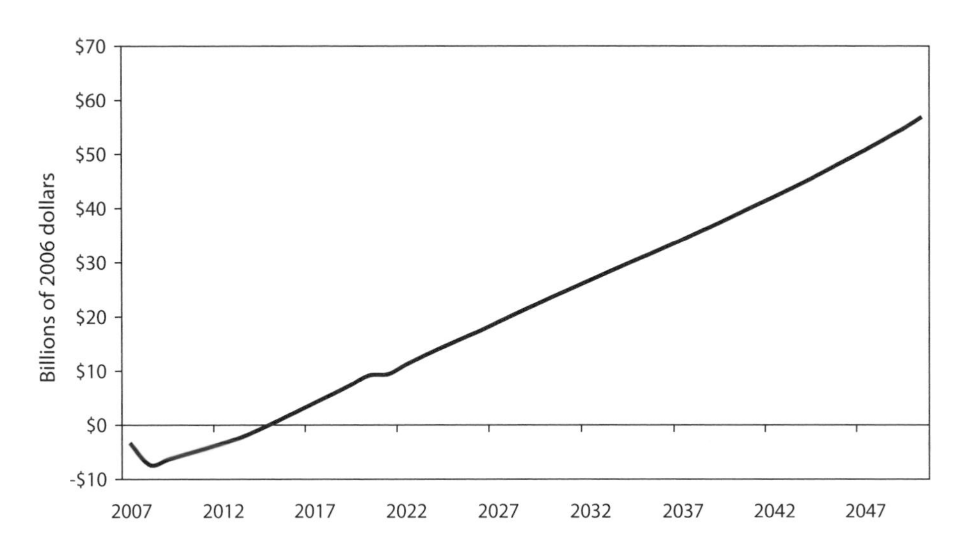

Source: Author's analysis.

Approximately 38% of the total budgetary benefits accrue to the federal government and 62% go to state and local governments. Thus, if the costs of the prekindergarten program were divided between the federal government and state and local governments in proportion to their shares of the budgetary benefits, all levels of government would experience, on average, more than three dollars of budget benefits for every dollar spent on the program in 2050.

But even if the federal government does not pay a large share of the additional costs of the prekindergarten program and simply maintains its efforts in Head Start and special education (allowing states to move some federal Head Start and special education funds into the program, redistributing federal pre-K commitments equitably among states, and holding states harmless from potential losses of federal pre-K funds),[28] the program will still be a worthwhile investment from the narrow perspective of state budgetary savings. States will, on average, experience net budget savings within 10 years (in 2016), and by 2050 every state tax dollar spent on the program will be offset by $2.15 in budgetary savings for state governments (see **Table 8**). In addition to state budget savings, in 2050 the federal government would be experiencing $29 billion in budget surplus.[29]

Similarly, even if state governments refuse to pay for a large share of the additional costs of the prekindergarten program and only maintain their efforts in Head Start, special education, and state pre-K, a federal program pays for itself over time. Under

TABLE 7 (Part 1 of 2) Government budget effects of targeted program, by state

	Additional taxpayer costs in 2008 (millions of 2006 dollars)	Years before annual budget benefits exceed annual costs	Total government surplus in 2050 (millions of 2006 dollars)	Ratio of government budget benefits to program costs in 2050
National	$8,197	9	$56,677	3.18
Alabama	$171	18	$434	1.95
Alaska	15	8	130	2.97
Arizona	247	11	1,735	2.84
Arkansas	78	8	577	3.36
California	1,311	9	8,593	3.17
Colorado	79	10	776	3.81
Connecticut	22	4	562	6.34
Delaware	4	4	96	7.25
District of Columbia	44	8	250	2.82
Florida	591	9	3,836	2.86
Georgia	316	9	2,264	3.04
Hawaii	18	8	164	4.10
Idaho	42	11	263	3.00
Illinois	343	9	2,165	3.23
Indiana	211	17	731	2.22
Iowa	67	10	360	3.17
Kansas	65	8	476	3.67
Kentucky	72	5	955	4.82
Louisiana	139	10	717	2.94
Maine	14	7	133	4.01
Maryland	103	9	890	3.52
Massachusetts	79	8	622	3.48
Michigan	207	7	1,798	3.92
Minnesota	32	5	836	6.70
Mississippi	105	10	522	2.90

TABLE 7 (Part 2 of 2) Government budget effects of targeted program, by state

	Additional taxpayer costs in 2008 (millions of 2006 dollars)	Years before annual budget benefits exceed annual costs	Total government surplus in 2050 (millions of 2006 dollars)	Ratio of government budget benefits to program costs in 2050
Missouri	$144	9	$888	3.25
Montana	19	7	123	3.28
Nebraska	40	9	252	3.35
Nevada	73	12	493	2.58
New Hampshire	13	9	108	3.62
New Jersey	74	7	894	4.18
New Mexico	68	10	369	3.05
New York	569	7	4,326	3.68
North Carolina	313	11	1,596	2.37
North Dakota	5	5	75	5.70
Ohio	190	7	1,904	4.32
Oklahoma	70	11	440	3.02
Oregon	66	8	688	3.64
Pennsylvania	298	9	1,833	3.29
Rhode Island	29	9	169	3.12
South Carolina	141	10	668	2.62
South Dakota	18	8	128	3.54
Tennessee	184	10	949	2.58
Texas	943	12	5,610	2.67
Utah	68	13	462	3.05
Vermont	2.5	4	64	5.92
Virginia	169	13	872	2.57
Washington	129	10	1,112	3.24
West Virginia	31	6	204	3.43
Wisconsin	126	8	1,010	3.69
Wyoming	7	7	65	4.51

Source: Author's analysis.

TABLE 8 (Part 1 of 2) **State-by-state government budget effects of a state-funded targeted program with federal maintenance of effort**

	Years before annual budget benefits exceed annual costs	State government surplus in 2050 (millions of 2006 dollars)	Ratio of gov't. budget benefits to program costs in 2050	Ratio of total state benefits to state program costs in 2050	Federal government surplus in 2050 (millions of 2006 dollars)
National	10	$27,456	2.15	11.9	$29,221
Alabama	29	$70	1.17	7.9	$364
Alaska	10	46	1.77	12.9	84
Arizona	16	660	1.75	11.1	1,075
Arkansas	8	315	2.52	12.7	262
California	11	3,648	1.96	11.2	4,945
Colorado	11	383	2.47	16.1	392
Connecticut	5	331	4.27	22.4	231
Delaware	4	56	4.97	28.8	40
District of Columbia	11	108	1.81	9.5	142
Florida	10	2,029	2.14	10.3	1,807
Georgia	10	1,182	2.25	11.9	1,082
Hawaii	11	71	2.46	16.9	93
Idaho	16	106	1.83	12.3	158
Illinois	11	1,012	2.08	11.8	1,152
Indiana	21	203	1.36	9.3	528
Iowa	12	154	1.97	12.4	206
Kansas	10	217	2.26	13.0	260
Kentucky	6	545	3.31	16.8	410
Louisiana	11	325	1.92	11.3	391
Maine	10	61	2.45	15.2	72
Maryland	10	433	2.27	12.7	457
Massachusetts	9	277	2.14	12.5	345
Michigan	8	908	2.55	12.9	890
Minnesota	6	493	4.55	26.0	343
Mississippi	14	187	1.73	11.8	335

TABLE 8 (Part 2 of 2) **State-by-state government budget effects of a state-funded targeted program with federal maintenance of effort**

	Years before annual budget benefits exceed annual costs	State government surplus in 2050 (millions of 2006 dollars)	Ratio of gov't. budget benefits to program costs in 2050	Ratio of total state benefits to state program costs in 2050	Federal government surplus in 2050 (millions of 2006 dollars)
Missouri	12	$338	1.88	11.5	$550
Montana	10	51	2.03	13.0	73
Nebraska	11	113	2.09	13.0	139
Nevada	14	209	1.73	10.9	284
New Hampshire	10	44	2.11	14.1	64
New Jersey	8	448	2.64	15.2	446
New Mexico	11	178	2.08	11.9	191
New York	8	2,522	2.62	11.2	1,805
North Carolina	12	750	1.75	9.3	846
North Dakota	8	40	3.79	24.3	35
Ohio	8	1,000	2.81	15.7	904
Oklahoma	16	165	1.83	13.0	275
Oregon	10	315	2.37	15.6	373
Pennsylvania	10	978	2.26	11.7	855
Rhode Island	11	80	2.03	10.8	89
South Carolina	11	299	1.82	9.9	369
South Dakota	11	55	2.16	13.5	73
Tennessee	11	385	1.67	8.5	564
Texas	12	2,540	1.95	12.7	3,069
Utah	17	182	1.84	12.9	280
Vermont	5	37	4.10	19.9	27
Virginia	14	293	1.58	10.2	578
Washington	12	504	2.08	12.2	607
West Virginia	8	93	2.18	11.1	111
Wisconsin	9	536	2.49	12.8	474
Wyoming	8	34	2.95	19.1	31

Source: Author's analysis.

these circumstances if the federal government pays most of the additional costs of the targeted program, then it will begin to experience net budget savings within 28 years, and by 2050 every federal tax dollar spent on the program will be offset by $1.60 in budgetary savings in that year for the federal government.[30] State governments collectively would experience $45 billion in budget surpluses by 2050.

Regardless of which level of government pays the costs of the prekindergarten program the total budgetary benefits to all levels of government remain unchanged—only the cost burden shifts. In the case of a federally funded program, states and localities receive their budget benefits without paying for most of the costs of the program, and in a states funded program, the federal government receives budget benefits without incurring most of the costs of the program. Our estimates show that the investment still pays for itself in the end and it is sensible for state governments or the federal government or both to invest in high-quality early childhood education.

State-by-state effects[31]

The state-by-state estimates capture variation in costs and benefits across states due to factors such as population, income distribution, teacher salaries, tax burdens, crime rates and current expenditures on all levels of education, child welfare, and criminal justice. All states eventually realize budget benefits from an investment in a high-quality, targeted pre-K program, but the timing and size of the benefits varies.

A fully phased-in, high-quality, targeted prekindergarten program in 2008, enrolling over 2 million children nationwide, would enroll as few as 2,000 children in the small state of Vermont and as many as 296,000 children in California. Given offsets for expenditures on Head Start, special education, and state pre-K, the program (which would cost taxpayers $8.2 billion nationwide) would cost taxpayers from as little as an additional $2.5 million in Vermont, and to as much as an additional $1.3 billion in California in 2008 (see Table 7).

Offsetting budget benefits (federal and state combined) outstrip costs nationwide within nine years, but at the state level timing varies substantially. The total (federal and state) offsetting budget benefits exceed costs in as little as four years (in 2010) for a program in Connecticut, Delaware, or Vermont or as many as 18 years (in 2024) in Alabama (see Table 7).

These differences in state budget benefits are driven by a multitude of factors. In general, states with greater current relative commitments to prekindergarten and other education programs, criminal justice programs, and child welfare programs, and those with higher tax burdens experience greater offsetting budget benefits than do other states. States with greater current commitments to prekindergarten programs need less additional public expenditure to finance the proposed high-quality pre-K program. Since the proposed prekindergarten program generates budget savings in special education, K-12 education, juvenile and adult criminal justice, and child welfare, states who are making larger financial commitments in education, justice, and child welfare save more money than states who are making smaller financial commitments in these areas.

Likewise, since the prospective pre-K program increases the future earnings of participants and their guardians, states with higher average pay and higher tax burdens will experience greater revenue increases than will states with lower average pay and lower tax burdens.

As noted above, by 2050, the last year estimated, the net nationwide budgetary surplus (federal and state combined) totals $57 billion. The corresponding state-level surpluses due to the program vary from $64 million and $65 million in Vermont and Wyoming, respectively, to $8.6 billion in California, $5.6 billion in Texas, and $4.3 billion in New York. Also as noted above, this yields a return to taxpayers averaging $3.18 nationwide for every tax dollar spent on a targeted prekindergarten program in 2050. The net budgetary benefit to state-level implementation is also favorable in every state. For example, by 2050, every dollar spent on the program in Alabama will be offset by $1.95 in budget savings in that year; and every dollar spent in Delaware will be offset by $7.25 in budget savings (see Table 7).

If the federal government refuses to pay the costs of the prekindergarten program and only maintains its efforts, allowing states to apply federal savings in Head Start and special education to offset some of the costs of the program (redistributing these federal commitments equitably among states and holding states harmless from potential losses of federal funds), the program is still a worthwhile investment from the narrow perspective of state budgetary savings. States experience net budget savings within as few as four years in Delaware and in no more than 29 years in Alabama.[32] By 2050, every state dollar spent on the program is offset by at least $1.17 in budgetary savings in the same year for Alabama and as much as $4.97 in budget savings for Delaware. And, in 2050 the federal government would be experiencing over $29 billion in budget surplus due to the pre-K investment made by states (see Table 8).[33]

Of course, if the federal government picked up the costs for the prekindergarten program, then state budgets would benefit enormously whether or not states maintained their efforts in pre-K, Head Start, and special education. If the federal government paid for the program and states simply maintained their efforts, then collectively state governments would experience $45 billion in budget surpluses by 2050.

Whether or not programs result in budgetary surpluses is not the most appropriate metric by which to judge their worthiness. Most government expenditures do not create offsetting receipts to the extent that early childhood education does and, indeed, it may be rare to find public programs that pay for themselves at the budgetary level. Even if eventual budget benefits did not outweigh costs, investment in early childhood education would create benefits to citizens through myriad non-revenue related effects. But, it is striking that either a federally funded or a state-funded national program will have significant positive effects on long-term state budget outlooks. Thus, these prekindergarten initiatives should be seen as sound investments on the part of government that generate substantial long-term benefits and not simply as programs requiring expenditures.

Economic effects

The previous section described the fiscal impacts of investment in a targeted pre-K program. It is important to keep in mind that savings to government are not the only benefits from prekindergarten investment, and it would be foolish to judge the merits of such investment solely in terms of its budgetary effects. In general, government investments may have impacts on the quality of life of citizens that justify their expense even if their net costs are very large. For example, our national defense program, which generates hundreds of billions of dollars annually in budget deficits, may be justified by the collective security that it provides us.

The benefits of prekindergarten include impacts on the health and well-being of citizens, the earnings of workers, crime rates, global competitiveness, and numerous other factors. Many of these other benefits may not be readily defined or measured in financial terms, just as the value of collective security may be difficult to monetize. But these other benefits still exist. Some of the non-budgetary benefits of pre-K are, however, measurable in dollar terms. Indeed, benefits that did not accrue to government finances but were measurable represented a sizeable portion of the total benefits found in studies of high-quality prekindergarten programs. In fact, 59% of the estimated total benefits found for the Chicago Child-Parent Centers program and 81.4% of the total benefits of the Perry Preschool program went to groups aside from government.[34]

These other measurable benefits come in many forms. For example, there are huge benefits to society from lower crime rates that go beyond just savings to governments. Fewer people will be robbed, raped, murdered, and assaulted. These benefits are quantified in the next section.

Another major benefit of pre-K investment is its impact on the future earnings of participants as a result of the higher educational attainment and other benefits of preschool for its participants. Moreover, the parents or guardians of participants are likely to experience increases in earnings since they will have more time for employment as a consequence of the free day care provided to their children by the prekindergarten program. In the long run these higher future earnings are very substantial.

Figure E illustrates the impact of targeted pre-K on the economy by showing the increase in compensation (wages plus fringe benefits) due to preschool investment. The initial increase in earnings and compensation occurs in 2007 when some of the guardians of prekindergarten participants take advantage of the subsidized child care provided by the program and enter the labor force. Later, in 2022, when the first cohort of participating children turns 18 and enters the labor market there is a sharp increase in earnings and compensation. By 2050, the increase in compensation due to pre-K investment is estimated to amount to $156 billion. This averages to an increase in compensation of $4,611 (in 2006 dollars) for each pre-K participant plus an increase in average compensation of $1,195 (in 2006 dollars) for the guardians of each pre-K participant in 2050.

The increased compensation for guardians estimated here is likely to be conservative, as we assume that guardians gain only during the two years in which their child is enrolled in prekindergarten. In reality, two additional years of labor-force participation

FIGURE E Annual compensation effect of targeted prekindergarten

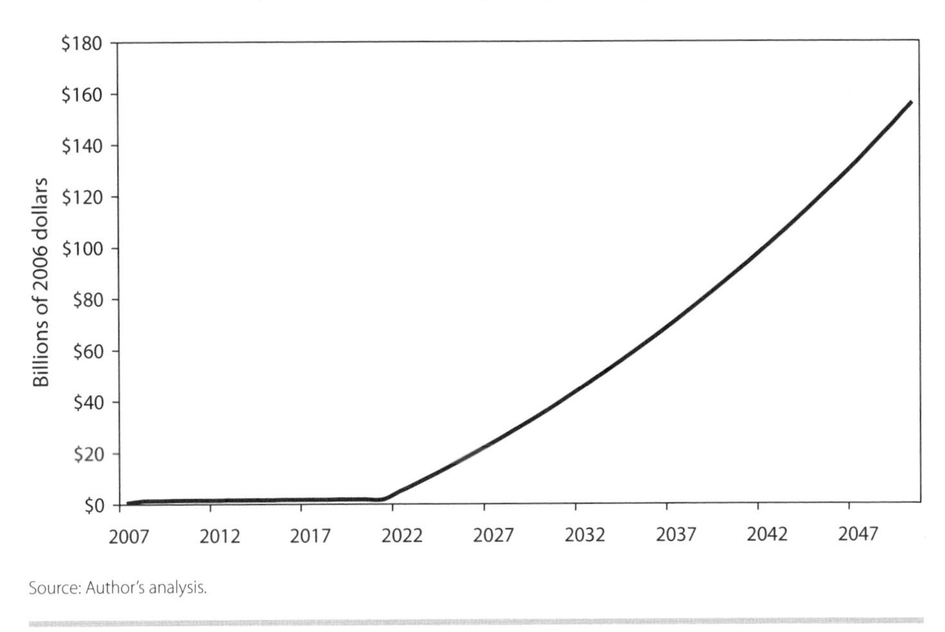

Source: Author's analysis.

early in a career is likely to have beneficial earnings effects for the rest of a worker's life. These increased earnings are not captured in the above estimates.

State-by-state compensation gains

By 2050, the increase in compensation due to pre-K investment is estimated to vary from about $154 million in Vermont and Wyoming to $25.7 billion in California (see Table 6). The average increase in compensation per each prekindergarten participant varies from $3,379 (in 2006 dollars) in West Virginia to $5,946 in New Hampshire. The increase in the average compensation of the guardians of pre-K participants varies from $700 in West Virginia to $1,232 in New Hampshire (all expressed in 2006 dollars).

Total state-by-state differences in compensation gains are largely due to differences in population, with large population states experiencing greater total compensation gains than small population states. However, state-by-state variations in compensation gains are also due in part to the fact that state-by-state earnings were adjusted to reflect average annual pay variation by state. Thus, states with relatively high average annual pay experience larger compensation gains per pre-K participant and their guardians than do states with relatively low average annual pay.

FIGURE F Crime savings due to targeted program, public and private

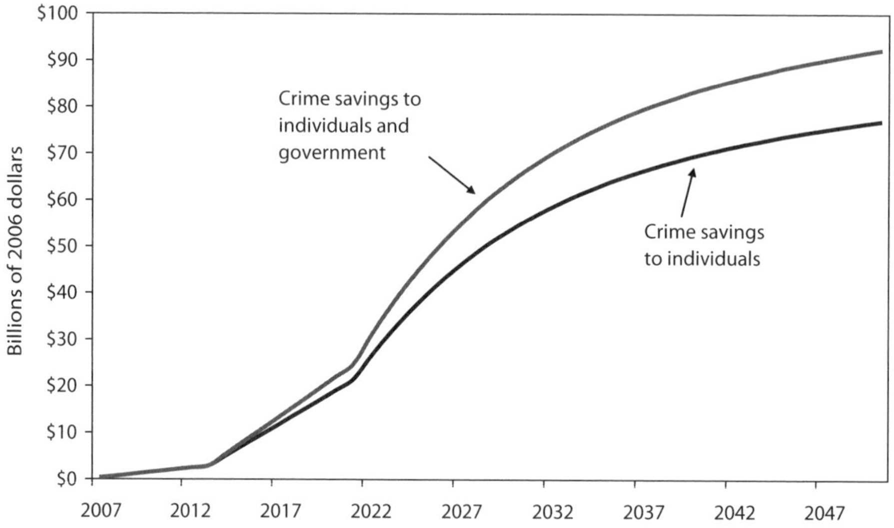

Source: Author's analysis.

Crime effects

Investments in pre-K programs are likely to substantially reduce crime rates and the extraordinary costs to society of criminality. Some of these reduced costs are savings to government in the form of lower criminal justice system costs. These savings to government would total nearly $15.4 billion in 2050 and were included in our earlier discussion of the fiscal effects of pre-k investments.

But there are other savings to society from reduced crime. These include the value of material losses and the pain and suffering that would otherwise be experienced by the victims of juvenile crime, adult crime, and child abuse and neglect.[35] By 2050, these savings to individuals from less crime would amount to $77 billion. Including the savings to government, the savings to society from reductions in criminality due to investments in prekindergarten programs would total $92 billion. **Figure F** illustrates the benefits to individuals and to society from pre-K induced reductions in crime.

State-by-state crime savings

The criminal justice savings to state governments would total $13.1 billion in 2050 and were included in our earlier discussion of the fiscal effects of pre-K investments. These state government savings from less crime would vary from $5.5 million in Vermont to $1.7 billion in Texas. By 2050, the savings to individuals from less crime and child abuse would amount to $34 million in Vermont and $9.8 billion and $9.9 billion in California and Texas, respectively (see Table 6).

Crime savings will tend to be larger in large population states, where there are more total crimes, than in small population states, where there are fewer total crimes. But variations in state-by-state crime savings are also due in part to variations in current state financial commitments to criminal justice and child welfare. States that are spending relatively more on their criminal justice system and on their child welfare programs stand to save relatively more than states that make smaller relative commitments in these areas. Similarly, savings to individuals from less crime and child abuse will tend to be greater in states with relatively high crime and child abuse rates than in states with relatively low crime and child abuse rates states.

Appendix A discusses costs and benefits that have been omitted in this analysis. As described in more detail in Appendix A, the benefits that we were not able to quantify in dollar terms are likely to be much greater than the omitted costs. Thus, the overall benefits and the benefit-cost ratio of a targeted pre-K education program are likely to be higher than those we have calculated and presented in this book.

The next chapter discusses the budgetary, economic, and crime effects of investment in a voluntary, high-quality, universal, publicly funded prekindergarten education program.

CHAPTER 3

The effects of investment in a voluntary, high-quality, publicly funded, universal prekindergarten education program on future government finances, the economy, and crime

Before describing the effects of a voluntary, high-quality, publicly funded, universal prekindergarten program on future government finances, the economy, and crime, several caveats are in order. First, we have less confidence in our estimates of the costs and benefits of a universal pre-K program than we do for those of a targeted program. Second, although the total benefits and costs are likely to be much larger, the benefits per participant and the overall benefit/cost ratio are likely to be smaller for a universal program than for a targeted program. However, it is not clear how much larger the total benefits are likely to be nor is it certain how much smaller the benefits per participant and the benefit/cost ratio are likely to be. Thus, the estimated outcomes of a universal program must be expressed more tentatively than those of a targeted program. The reasons for these caveats are explained below and in more detail in Appendix B.

Numerous studies have examined the long-term effects of prekindergarten and other early childhood development programs on the outcomes of participating children. However, most of these studies have focused on relatively poor children and children at high risk for educational failure. Prekindergarten and other ECD programs that have served children from middle- and upper-income families have generally not been subject to carefully controlled studies with long-term follow up of participants and a control group of non-participants. Thus, the costs and benefits of prekindergarten programs that include middle- and upper-income children cannot be estimated with as much precision as can the costs and benefits of pre-K programs serving relatively poor children only. Given the greater uncertainty about the returns to non-poor children relative to poor children from ECD investment, the costs and benefits of a universal prekindergarten program are less sure than those for a more targeted prekindergarten program.

There are good reasons to expect that a universal program, while it may generate enormous benefits, will not generate the same magnitude of benefits *per participant* or the same high rate of return as a program targeted to relatively disadvantaged children. There are reasons to believe that the benefits of a high-quality prekindergarten program like the Chicago CPC program, which served high-risk children (from low-income families), *will not apply fully* to medium-risk children (from middle-income families) and low-risk children (from high-income families) who would otherwise attend no prekindergarten. In addition, there are reasons to believe that the benefits of a program like the Chicago CPC, which compared outcomes for children who attended a high-quality prekindergarten program to outcomes for children who (for the most part) attended no prekindergarten, *will not apply fully* to children who would otherwise attend some form of preschool education program. Children who are likely to enroll in a universal program may be somewhat more likely to otherwise attend some form of preschool education than are children who are likely to enroll in a targeted program. Thus the benefits per participant and the overall benefit/cost ratio of a universal prekindergarten program are likely to be smaller than those of a more targeted prekindergarten program.

At the same time, of course, the total benefits of a universal program will be larger than those of a targeted program and the ratio of benefits to costs of a universal program, while smaller than that for a targeted program, may still be large enough to amply justify public investment in the universal program. But to estimate the costs and benefits of a universal prekindergarten program, we have to address the caveats described above. Specifically, we have to make two key evaluations:

1. To what extent will the benefits of a high-quality, prekindergarten program like the Chicago CPC program, which served high-risk children (from low income families), apply to medium-risk children (from middle-income families) and low-risk children (from high-income families) who would otherwise attend no prekindergarten?
2. To what extent will the benefits of a high-quality pre-K program like the Chicago CPC program, that compared outcomes for children who attended a high-quality prekindergarten program to outcomes for children who (for the most part) attended no pre-K, apply to children who would otherwise attend some form of prekindergarten?

As described in more detail in Appendix B, in answer to the first question the empirical research shows that all children—regardless of whether they are from poor, middle-income or upper-income families—benefit from high-quality prekindergarten. However, studies differ on the degree of impact that pre-K has on children from different economic backgrounds. Many studies find that the positive effects of prekindergarten on children from more and less advantaged backgrounds are nearly identical. Other studies suggest that children from low-income families gain more from pre-K than do children from middle- and high-income families. At least one study (Gormley et al. 2004) suggests that for some skills lower middle-income children gain more than poorer or wealthier children. Thus, we offer high, low, and intermediate (or most likely) range estimates of these possible effects. In the discussion below that describes the estimated costs and benefits of the universal prekindergarten program, the intermediate range estimates are used, but a sensitivity analysis is performed in Appendix A to demonstrate what effect different estimates have on the final results.

In answer to the second question, again discussed in greater detail in Appendix B, the literature shows that there is evidence that existing prekindergarten programs (both private and public) provide important benefits to participants compared to children who attend no prekindergarten. In addition, higher quality pre-K programs provide greater benefits than lower quality pre-K programs. Hence, children moving from low- or medium-quality prekindergarten to high-quality prekindergarten should not gain as much as children moving from no pre-K to high-quality pre-K. However, given that there is little quantitative evidence to indicate exactly how much smaller the impacts of currently existing prekindergarten programs would be compared to a prospective high-quality program, we provide a range of estimates: high, low, and intermediate (or most likely) estimates. In the estimates below of the costs and benefits of a voluntary, high-quality, universal prekindergarten program, we use the intermediate estimate, but the sensitivity analysis in Appendix A includes the full range of estimates.

The universal program, modeled on the Chicago CPC program, would be voluntary for all three- and four-year-old children.[36] Its estimated enrollment is described in Appendix B on methodology. Aside from the population of children it serves, we assume that the other characteristics of a universal, voluntary, high-quality, publicly funded pre-K program would be the same as those described for a targeted program in chapter two. Below, we translate the measured impacts of the Chicago CPC program into estimates of how public investment in a universal, high-quality, prekindergarten program would affect future government finances, the economy, and crime given the attenuations described above.

Total benefits

The annual budgetary, earnings, and crime benefits of a voluntary, high-quality, publicly funded, universal prekindergarten program would begin to outstrip the annual costs of the program within nine years and would do so by a growing margin every year thereafter. By the year 2050, the annual benefits would total $779 billion: $191 billion in government budget benefits, $432 billion in increased compensation of workers, and $156 billion in reduced costs to individuals from less crime and child abuse (**Table 9**). These annual benefits in 2050 would exceed the costs of the program in that year by a ratio of 8.2 to 1. Broken down by state, in 2050 the total annual benefits would outstrip the annual costs of the program by a minimum of 6.1 to 1 for residents of Alabama and by as much as 11.4 to 1 for the residents of Wyoming. The annual costs and budgetary, earnings, and crime benefits are further detailed below.

Budget effects

We examine the budget effects through the year 2050 of launching a permanent, voluntary, high-quality, universal prekindergarten program in 2007 for all three- and four-

TABLE 9 (Part 1 of 2) State-by-state costs and benefits of universal program, 2050

	Government budget benefits (millions of 2006 dollars)	Increased compensation (millions of 2006 dollars)	Savings to individuals from reduced crime (millions of 2006 dollars)	Total budget, compensation, and crime benefits in 2050 (millions of 2006 dollars)	Ratio of total annual benefits to program costs
National	$191,109	$431,959	$155,736	$778,804	8.2
Alabama	$1,795	$5,019	$997	$7,812	6.1
Alaska	527	1,502	474	2,503	7.8
Arizona	5,317	11,783	5,866	22,965	7.9
Arkansas	1,526	3,079	1,204	5,809	8.5
California	26,482	64,408	17,927	108,816	8.4
Colorado	3,418	8,183	4,070	15,670	9.4
Connecticut	2,088	5,060	1,257	8,405	9.1
Delaware	311	735	311	1,358	11.2
District of Columbia	591	1,164	505	2,260	8.1
Florida	12,607	24,153	10,499	47,259	7.4
Georgia	7,189	15,396	5,847	28,432	9.0
Hawaii	811	2,066	769	3,646	9.0
Idaho	991	2,286	1,263	4,540	8.7
Illinois	7,673	17,908	6,169	31,750	8.9
Indiana	3,250	8,427	3,168	14,844	7.0
Iowa	1,380	3,402	1,219	6,001	8.4
Kansas	1,616	3,683	1,339	6,638	8.9
Kentucky	2,322	4,599	2,115	9,036	10.0
Louisiana	2,273	5,077	2,317	9,667	8.4
Maine	500	1,180	456	2,136	9.1
Maryland	4,251	10,434	3,061	17,747	8.7
Massachusetts	3,126	8,636	1,461	13,224	7.6
Michigan	5,514	12,800	2,727	21,041	8.1
Minnesota	3,921	9,015	3,901	16,837	10.2
Mississippi	1,326	3,017	1,518	5,862	8.4

TABLE 9 (Part 2 of 2) State-by-state costs and benefits of universal program, 2050

	Government budget benefits (millions of 2006 dollars)	Increased compensation (millions of 2006 dollars)	Savings to individuals from reduced crime (millions of 2006 dollars)	Total budget, compensation, and crime benefits in 2050 (millions of 2006 dollars)	Ratio of total annual benefits to program costs
Missouri	$3,091	$7,575	$2,433	$13,099	8.2
Montana	386	894	418	1,699	8.0
Nebraska	990	2,400	998	4,388	8.6
Nevada	2,174	5,109	2,612	9,895	7.7
New Hampshire	715	2,078	507	3,299	8.6
New Jersey	5,261	13,633	3,362	22,255	10.5
New Mexico	1,037	2,241	1,006	4,284	9.0
New York	12,685	23,184	8,662	44,531	9.4
North Carolina	6,029	12,933	4,746	23,708	6.9
North Dakota	276	616	348	1,240	10.1
Ohio	6,178	13,953	5,204	25,336	8.8
Oklahoma	1,673	4,308	1,609	7,589	8.5
Oregon	2,221	5,174	2,481	9,875	8.2
Pennsylvania	6,447	13,965	5,580	25,992	8.3
Rhode Island	571	1,315	402	2,288	8.0
South Carolina	2,304	5,157	1,770	9,231	7.5
South Dakota	402	936	381	1,718	9.0
Tennessee	3,344	7,721	1,853	12,918	6.4
Texas	17,167	41,978	16,759	75,904	8.0
Utah	2,271	5,776	2,507	10,554	8.8
Vermont	273	668	99	1,040	9.3
Virginia	4,545	13,073	2,332	19,950	7.7
Washington	4,135	10,086	3,120	17,341	7.7
West Virginia	572	1,327	225	2,124	7.9
Wisconsin	3,408	7,486	2,489	13,383	9.5
Wyoming	238	540	317	1,095	11.4

Source: Author's analysis.

year-old children in America. For illustration purposes, we assume that the program would be fully phased in by 2008. We consider budget effects on the federal government, the combination of state and local governments, and on a state-by-state basis. Although responsibilities have shifted in the last half-century and will continue to do so over the nearly half-century time frame used in this study, we assume that all levels of government will share in the costs of education, criminal justice, and child welfare in the future in the same proportions as they are doing in the present. Likewise, we assume that federal, state, and local tax rates will remain constant over the time period analyzed in this study. All the costs and benefits are expressed in (real or inflation adjusted) 2006 dollars.

A high-quality, universal pre-K program would cost nearly $6,300 per participant and could be expected to enroll nearly 7 million children in 2008 when it is fully phased in, for a total cost to taxpayers of about $43.2 billion in 2008. However, some of this money is already being spent on related programs. For example, 38 states have publicly financed prekindergarten programs for children, some of whom would be enrolled in our proposed program. Similarly, all states and the federal government pay for special education and Head Start services for young children, some of whom would attend our proposed program. Hence, some of the current expenditures on state prekindergarten programs and some of the current expenditures on special education and Head Start services are for children who will be attending the proposed universal pre-K program. We assume that these expenditures, currently at about $10 billion, could be used to pay for part of the proposed program. As such, our proposed high-quality, universal prekindergarten program would require approximately $33.3 billion in *additional* government outlays in 2008 once it is fully phased in.

Government costs will initially reflect only the actual expenditures on the pre-K program. Eventually there will be some additional government expenditures due to the increased educational attainment of pre-K participants. Increased public high school costs appear when the first cohort of participants turns 17, and increased higher education costs appear when the first cohort turns 18.

The offsetting budget savings begin small but grow rapidly over time and eventually outstrip the costs. Budget savings in the first year of the program will manifest themselves as reductions in child welfare expenditures as fewer children will be the victims of child abuse and neglect. In addition, some parents will take advantage of the fact that part of their child care needs will be covered by the prekindergarten program by entering the labor force, securing employment, and paying more in taxes. When the pre-K participants enter the K-12 public school system, additional budget savings will begin to appear, as these children will be less likely to repeat a grade or need expensive special education services. When the first cohort of children turns 10 further budget savings will begin to be realized as lower juvenile crime rates will require less expenditure on the juvenile justice system. As adults, the prekindergarten participants will be less engaged in crime and earn more income. Thus there will eventually be savings to the adult criminal justice system and increased tax revenue derived from the labor of pre-K participants.

FIGURE G Total budget costs and benefits of universal program

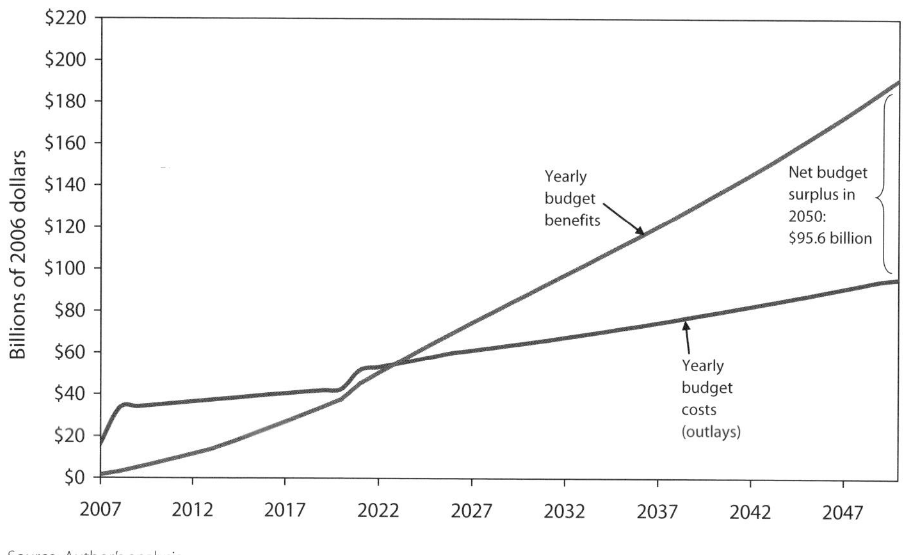

Source: Author's analysis.

Offsetting budget benefits take a while to outstrip the costs, but the gap becomes substantially favorable over time. For the first 16 years of a national universal prekindergarten program, costs exceed offsetting budget benefits, but by a declining margin. Thereafter, starting in 2023, offsetting budget benefits exceed costs by a growing margin each year. This pattern is illustrated in **Figures G** and **H**. Annual costs and benefits are portrayed in real (inflation-adjusted) terms in Figure 7. Figure 8 shows the annual net budget impact in real terms.

In the second year of the program, 2008, when the program is fully phased in, government outlays exceed offsetting budget benefits by $30.4 billion. The universal pre-K program-related deficit shrinks for the next 14 years. By the 17th year of the program, in 2023, the deficit turns into a surplus that grows every year thereafter culminating in a net budgetary surplus of some $96 billion in 2050, the last year estimated, as illustrated in Figure H. Thus by 2050, every dollar spent on the program by taxpayers is offset by $2.00 in budget savings in that year.

The reason for this fiscal pattern is as follows. The costs of the program grow fairly slowly for the first decade and a half, in tandem with inflation and modest growth in the population of three- and four-year-old participants. Thereafter, costs grow at a somewhat faster pace for a few years as, in addition to the costs of educating three- and four-year olds, the first and subsequent cohorts of participant children begin to use

FIGURE H Net benefits to government budgets from universal program

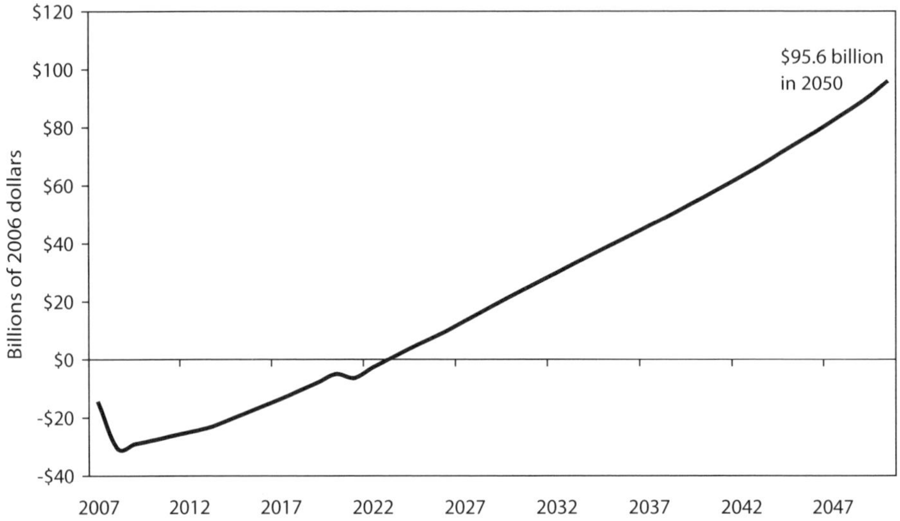

Source: Author's analysis.

more high school and public higher-education services. Budget benefits during the first two years result from reductions in child welfare spending due to lower rates of child maltreatment and from increased taxes on the earnings of parents due to subsidized child care. After the first two years, when the first cohort of children start entering the public school system, public education expenditures begin to diminish due to less grade retention and need for special education. After a decade and half, the first cohort of children begins entering the workforce, resulting in increased earnings and thus higher tax revenues. In addition, governments eventually experience lower judicial system costs due to less juvenile and, later, adult crime, starting when the first cohort of participants reaches age 10.

Approximately 42% of the total budgetary benefits from a universal program accrue to the federal government and 58% go to state and local governments. Thus, if the costs of the program were divided between the federal government and state and local governments in proportion to their shares of the budgetary benefits, then all levels of government would experience two dollars of budget savings for every dollar spent on the program in 2050.

But if the federal government refused to share proportionally to its benefits in the costs of the universal program and simply maintained its efforts in Head Start and special education and allowed states to apply federal savings in Head Start and special education to offset some of the costs of the program (redistributing federal pre-K commitments equitably among states and holding states harmless from potential losses of federal funds), the universal program would still be a worthwhile investment from the narrow perspective of state budgetary savings for most states.[37] States as a whole would experience net budget savings within 23 years (in 2029) and by 2050, every tax dollar spent on the program would be offset by $1.26 in budgetary savings for state governments. In 2050, the federal government would be enjoying $73 billion in surpluses.

If state governments refused to pay in proportion to their benefits for the costs of the prekindergarten program and only maintained their efforts in Head Start, special education, and state preschool and allowed the federal government to apply state savings in Head Start, special education, and state prekindergarten to offset some of the costs of the program, the universal program will return $1.02 in budget savings in 2050 for every federal tax dollar spent in that year. Of course, if the federal government were paying for the bulk of the program, state governments would be enjoying enormous surpluses of $94 billion in 2050.[38]

State-by-state budget effects[39]

Our state-by-state estimates capture variation in costs and benefits across states due to factors such as population, income distribution, teacher salaries, crime rates, tax burdens, and current expenditures on all levels of education, child welfare, and criminal justice. All states eventually realize budget benefits from a universal prekindergarten investment, but the timing and size of the benefits varies.

A high-quality, universal prekindergarten program enrolling nearly 7 million children nationwide would enroll as few as 10,600 children in the small state of Vermont and more than 870,000 children in the large state of California in 2008 when it is fully phased in. Given offsets for expenditures on Head Start, special education, and state prekindergarten, the program (which would cost $33.3 billion nationwide) would cost from as little as an additional $38 million in Vermont to as much as an additional $4.6 billion in California in 2008 (see **Table 10**).

Offsetting budget benefits (federal and state combined) outstrip costs nationwide within 17 years, but at the state level, timing varies substantially. The total (federal and state) offsetting budget benefits exceed costs-by-state in as little as 10 years (in 2016) in Kentucky and New York and in as many as 29 years (in 2035) in Alabama (see Table 10).

These differences in state budget benefits are driven by a multitude of factors. In general, states with greater current relative commitments to pre-K and other education programs, criminal justice programs, and child welfare programs, and those with higher tax burdens experience greater offsetting budget benefits than do other states. States with greater current commitments to state prekindergarten programs need less additional public expenditure to finance the proposed high-quality pre-K program than do states with larger current commitments to state pre-K programs. Since the proposed prekindergarten program generates budget savings in special education, K-12 education, juvenile and adult criminal justice, and child welfare, states that are making larger financial commitments in education, justice, and child welfare save more money than

TABLE 10 (Part 1 of 2) Government budget effects of universal program, by state

	Additional taxpayer costs in 2008 (millions of 2006 dollars)	Years before annual budget benefits exceed annual costs	Total government surplus in 2050 (millions of 2006 dollars)	Ratio of government budget benefits to program costs in 2050
National	$33,338	17	$95,605	2.00
Alabama	$512	29	$518	1.41
Alaska	89	21	206	1.64
Arizona	805	20	2,411	1.83
Arkansas	238	12	844	2.24
California	4,631	17	13,586	2.05
Colorado	560	19	1,749	2.05
Connecticut	349	17	1,159	2.25
Delaware	60	11	190	2.56
District of Columbia	95	12	312	2.12
Florida	1,894	14	6,258	1.99
Georgia	946	13	4,020	2.27
Hawaii	176	20	408	2.01
Idaho	181	19	468	1.90
Illinois	1,392	17	4,101	2.15
Indiana	800	25	1,135	1.54
Iowa	319	19	666	1.93
Kansas	306	16	867	2.16
Kentucky	328	10	1,418	2.57
Louisiana	477	17	1,119	1.97
Maine	95	17	265	2.12
Maryland	668	18	2,212	2.08
Massachusetts	660	22	1,387	1.80
Michigan	1,052	16	2,902	2.11
Minnesota	567	17	2,267	2.37
Mississippi	299	18	629	1.90

TABLE 10 (Part 2 of 2) Government budget effects of universal program, by state

	Additional taxpayer costs in 2008 (millions of 2006 dollars)	Years before annual budget benefits exceed annual costs	Total government surplus in 2050 (millions of 2006 dollars)	Ratio of government budget benefits to program costs in 2050
Missouri	$634	18	$1,498	1.94
Montana	88	17	174	1.82
Nebraska	212	19	481	1.94
Nevada	318	22	894	1.70
New Hampshire	135	21	331	1.87
New Jersey	702	14	3,148	2.49
New Mexico	198	14	559	2.17
New York	1,784	10	7,932	2.67
North Carolina	970	21	2,575	1.75
North Dakota	55	16	154	2.26
Ohio	1,203	16	3,287	2.14
Oklahoma	328	21	780	1.87
Oregon	367	19	1,019	1.85
Pennsylvania	1,277	17	3,319	2.06
Rhode Island	114	18	285	1.99
South Carolina	442	17	1,075	1.88
South Dakota	77	16	211	2.10
Tennessee	669	21	1,325	1.66
Texas	2,928	20	7,671	1.81
Utah	393	22	1,069	1.89
Vermont	38	13	160	2.43
Virginia	847	24	1,957	1.76
Washington	673	22	1,888	1.84
West Virginia	120	11	303	2.12
Wisconsin	527	14	2,003	2.43
Wyoming	44	13	142	2.47

Source: Author's analysis.

TABLE 11 (Part 1 of 2) State-by-state government budget effects of a state-funded universal program with federal maintenance of effort

	Years before annual budget benefits exceed annual costs	State government surplus in 2050 (millions of 2006 dollars)	Ratio of state government budget benefits to program costs in 2050	Ratio of total state benefits to state program costs in 2050	Federal government surplus in 2050 (millions of 2006 dollars)
National	23	$23,053	1.26	7.9	$72,552
Alabama	*	$-241	0.79	5.9	$760
Alaska	*	-34	0.88	7.7	240
Arizona	35	227	1.08	7.6	2,183
Arkansas	16	298	1.48	8.3	546
California	24	2,783	1.23	8.1	10,803
Colorado	24	408	1.27	9.3	1,341
Connecticut	20	366	1.42	8.7	794
Delaware	12	66	1.59	10.9	123
District of Columbia	18	95	1.36	7.8	217
Florida	20	1,876	1.32	7.2	4,381
Georgia	18	1,348	1.46	8.7	2,672
Hawaii	29	63	1.17	8.9	345
Idaho	29	68	1.14	8.5	400
Illinois	21	1,137	1.34	8.6	2,964
Indiana	*	-215	0.89	6.8	1,350
Iowa	27	113	1.17	8.2	554
Kansas	22	219	1.32	8.5	648
Kentucky	12	591	1.71	9.8	827
Louisiana	22	275	1.26	8.2	844
Maine	23	60	1.28	8.8	204
Maryland	23	537	1.28	8.4	1,675
Massachusetts	41	60	1.04	7.2	1,328
Michigan	21	805	1.33	7.8	2,097
Minnesota	19	782	1.51	9.9	1,485
Mississippi	28	82	1.13	8.3	546
Missouri	32	164	1.11	7.8	1,335

TABLE 11 (Part 2 of 2) State-by-state government budget effects of a state-funded universal program with federal maintenance of effort

	Years before annual budget benefits exceed annual costs	State government surplus in 2050 (millions of 2006 dollars)	Ratio of state government budget benefits to program costs in 2050	Ratio of total state benefits to state program costs in 2050	Federal government surplus in 2050 (millions of 2006 dollars)
Montana	25	$15	1.08	8.0	$159
Nebraska	27	79	1.17	8.3	401
Nevada	41	36	1.03	7.5	858
New Hampshire	44	1	1.00	8.3	331
New Jersey	19	966	1.49	10.1	2,181
New Mexico	18	189	1.44	9.1	370
New York	11	3,882	1.88	9.1	4,050
North Carolina	32	413	1.13	6.7	2,162
North Dakota	19	46	1.41	10.1	108
Ohio	21	932	1.35	8.5	2,355
Oklahoma	35	82	1.10	8.5	698
Oregon	32	105	1.10	8.1	914
Pennsylvania	18	1,075	1.37	8.1	2,244
Rhode Island	23	71	1.27	7.7	214
South Carolina	26	204	1.18	7.3	871
South Dakota	22	44	1.26	8.8	166
Tennessee	41	63	1.03	6.2	1,263
Texas	34	694	1.08	7.8	6,976
Utah	35	125	1.11	8.6	944
Vermont	14	56	1.54	9.0	105
Virginia	*	-67	0.97	7.4	2,025
Washington	34	279	1.14	7.5	1,609
West Virginia	13	77	1.31	7.6	226
Wisconsin	17	773	1.59	9.3	1,230
Wyoming	14	47	1.54	11.2	94

* Program budget benefits do not exceed costs within the window of this analysis

Source: Author's analysis.

states that are making smaller financial commitments in these areas. Likewise, since the prospective pre-K program increases the future earnings of participants and their guardians, states with higher average pay and higher tax burdens will experience greater revenues increases than will states with lower average pay and lower tax burdens.

As noted above, by 2050, the net nationwide budgetary surplus (federal and state combined) totals $96 billion. The corresponding state-level surpluses due to the program vary from $142 million in Wyoming to $13.6 billion in California. Also as noted above, this yields a return to taxpayers averaging $2.00 in offsetting budget benefits for every dollar spent on the program nationwide in 2050. The total return to state-level implementation is also favorable for every state. For example, by 2050, for every dollar being spent on the program in that year, a program in Alabama will create $1.41 in budget savings and every dollar invested in the program in New York would return to taxpayers $2.67 in budget savings (see Table 10).

If the federal government refuses to pay for a significant share of the costs of the prekindergarten program and only maintains its current efforts, allowing states to apply federal savings in Head Start and special education to offset some of the costs of the program (redistributing federal Head Start commitments equitably among states and holding states harmless from potential losses of federal funds), the program generates budget surpluses in 46 states by 2050. Collectively, states experience net budget savings in 23 years (2029) with an average return per state tax dollar expended on the program of $1.26 in 2050, but the returns per state tax dollar vary from a low of 79 cents in Alabama to a high of $1.88 in New York in 2050, while the federal government would be enjoying $73 billion in budget surplus due to the prekindergarten investment made largely by states (see **Table 11**).[40]

It is important to understand that the ratio of government budget benefits to program costs in 2050 is a cash analysis that compares the net government expenditure impact of the program to the additional taxpayer costs engendered by the program in 2050. Thus, for a publicly financed pre-K program, the government budget/cost ratio considers all the additional costs due to the program but only the additional government budgetary benefits of the program, thereby ignoring the compensation, crime, and other benefits of the program. The individual state government budget/cost ratios in Table 11 indicate that from the taxpayers' perspective *alone*, the program fully pays for itself in 2050 in 46 states.

This is an extraordinary finding: it is rare to find government expenditures on a program creating offsetting budget savings such that the public program pays for itself at the budgetary level. Of course, once we add in the other benefits of the program, the universal pre-K program, like the targeted program discussed in the previous chapter, amply pays for itself in all 50 states. Indeed, the ratio of total state benefits to state program costs in 2050, when states pay for most of the universal program and the federal government simply maintains its current efforts in prekindergarten, varies from a minimum ratio of 5.9 to 1 in Alabama to 11.2 in Wyoming (see Table 11). In fact, the non-budgetary benefits of the pre-K program are by themselves much greater than the costs of the program in all 50 states. Consequently, the budget benefits, even those in

FIGURE I Annual compensation effect of universal program

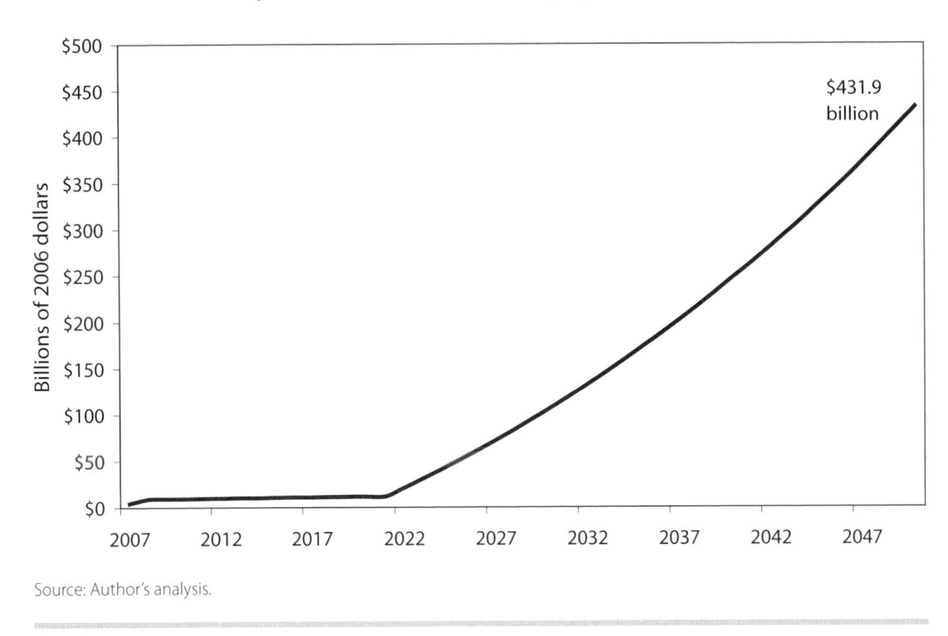

Source: Author's analysis.

the few states where the budget benefits do not exceed the additional costs of the program in 2050 when states pay for most of the program, should be seen as bonuses that are in addition to the other non-budgetary benefits.

Economic effects

As was noted both above and in the previous chapter, savings to government budgets are not the only benefits from prekindergarten investment, and it would be unwise to judge the merits of such investment solely in terms of its budgetary effects. Government investments may affect the quality of life of citizens that justify their expense even if their net costs are very large. For example, our investments in state and national parks cost billions of dollars annually, but may be justified by the enjoyment they provide visitors.

Not all the benefits of prekindergarten may be measured in financial terms, just as the value our national parks may be difficult to monetize. But at least some of the non-budgetary benefits of pre-K education are measurable in dollar terms.

Among the other quantifiable benefits of prekindergarten investment are its impact on the future earnings of participants and the guardians of participants. **Figure I** illustrates the impact of a universal pre-K program on the economy by showing the increase in compensation (wages plus fringe benefits) due to prekindergarten investment. The initial increase in earnings and compensation occurs in 2007 when some of the guardians of pre-K participants take advantage of the subsidized child care provided by the pre-K program and enter the labor force. Later, in 2022, when the first cohort of participating children turns 18 and enters the labor market, there is a sharp increase in earnings and compensation. By 2050, the increase in compensation due to prekindergarten investment is estimated to amount to 1.8% of the gross domestic product (GDP) or $432 billion. This averages to an increase in compensation of $3,817 (in 2006 dollars) for each pre-K participant plus an increase in average compensation of $2,295 (in 2006 dollars) for the guardians of each prekindergarten participant.

The increased compensation for guardians estimated here is likely to be conservative, as we assume that guardians gain only during the two years in which their child is enrolled. In reality, two additional years of labor-force participation early in a career are likely to generate beneficial earnings effects for the rest of a worker's life. The above estimates do not capture these increased earnings.

State-by-state compensation gains

By 2050, the increase in compensation due to universal prekindergarten investment is estimated to vary from $540 million in Wyoming to over $64.4 billion in California (see Table 9). The average increase in compensation per each pre-K participant in 2050 varies from $2,885 (in 2006 dollars) in West Virginia to $4,609 in New Hampshire. The increase in the average compensation of the guardians of pre-K participants in 2050 varies from $1,682 in West Virginia to $2,960 in New Hampshire (both expressed in 2006 dollars).

Total state-by-state differences in compensations gains are largely due to differences in population, with large population states experiencing greater total compensation gains than small population states. However, these variations in gains occur partially because state-by-state earnings were adjusted to reflect average annual pay variation by state. Thus, states with relatively high average annual pay experience larger compensation gains per pre-K participant and their guardians than do states with relatively low average annual pay.

Crime effects

Investments in a universal prekindergarten program are likely to substantially reduce crime rates and the extraordinary costs to society of criminality. Some of these reduced costs are savings to government in the form of lower criminal justice system costs. These savings to government would total about $32.3 billion in 2050 and were included in our earlier discussion of the fiscal effects of universal pre-K investment.

There are more savings to society from reduced crime. These include the value of material losses and the pain and suffering that would otherwise be experienced by the victims of juvenile crime, adult crime, and child abuse and neglect. By 2050, the savings to individuals from less crime amount to $155.7 billion. Including the savings

FIGURE J Crime savings due to universal program, public and private

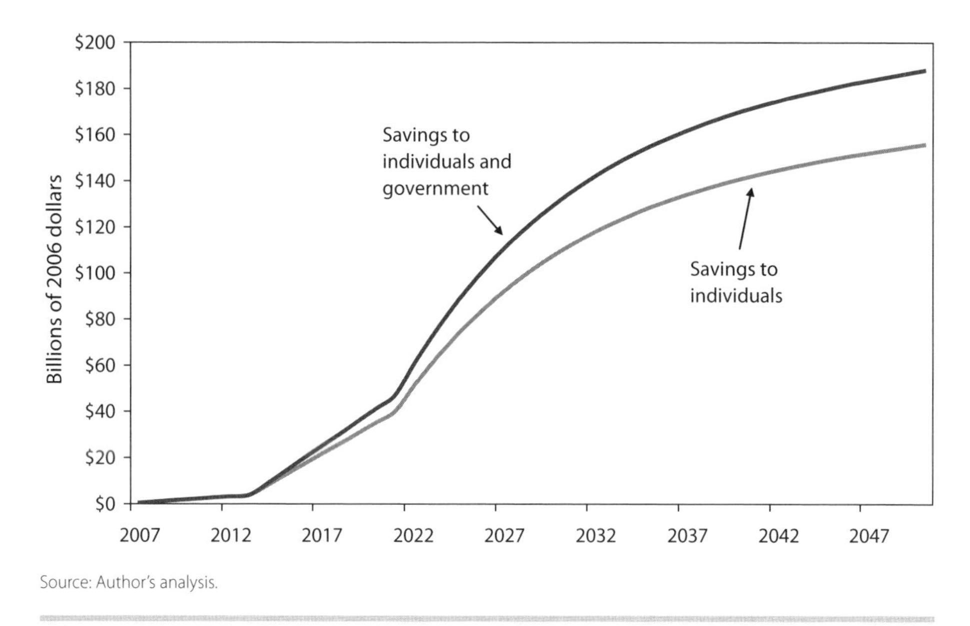

Source: Author's analysis.

to government, the savings to society from reduced crime total $188 billion. **Figure J** illustrates the benefits to individuals and to society from prekindergarten-induced reductions in crime.

State-by-state crime savings

The criminal justice savings to state governments total $27.5 billion in 2050 and were included in our earlier discussion of the fiscal effects of universal pre-K investment. These state government savings from less crime would vary from $16.9 million in Vermont to over $3.1 billion in California. By 2050, the savings to individuals from less crime and child abuse amount to $99 million in Vermont and to $17.9 billion in California (see Table 9).

Crime savings will tend to be larger in large population states, where there are more total crimes, than in small population states, where there are fewer total crimes. However, variations in state-by-state crime savings are also due in part to variations in current state financial commitments to criminal justice and child welfare. States that are spending relatively more on their criminal justice system and on their child welfare programs stand to save relatively more than states that make smaller relative commitments in these areas. Similarly, savings to individuals from less crime and child abuse will tend to be greater in states with relatively high crime and child abuse rates than in those with relatively low rates.

Aside from positive budget implications, earnings effects, and crime impacts, there are other benefits from a high-quality pre-K program that we have not evaluated. There may have been costs that we have omitted from our analysis, as well. Many of these costs and benefits are difficult to measure or to monetize. However, the benefits that we were not able to quantify in dollar terms are likely to be much greater than the omitted costs. Thus, the overall benefits and the benefit-cost ratio of a universal pre-K education program are likely to be higher than those we have calculated and presented in this chapter. These omitted costs and benefits are described in Appendix A.

Conclusion

Investment in high-quality prekindergarten can help the United States achieve a multitude of social and economic development objectives. These include stronger economic growth, income growth, job creation, poverty and inequality reduction, education and health care improvement, and crime reduction. Moreover, high-quality pre-K helps to create the conditions that enable people to achieve their potential, live lives of dignity, and maximize their choices.

A high-quality, nationwide commitment to early childhood development would cost a significant amount of money upfront, but it would have a substantial payoff in the future. The U.S. political system, with its two- and four-year cycles, tends to under-invest in programs with long lags between when investment costs are incurred and when benefits are enjoyed. The fact that state and local governments cannot capture all the benefits of pre-K investment may also discourage them from assuming all the costs of pre-K programs. Yet, the economic case for public investment in prekindergarten is compelling.

We estimate that providing a voluntary, high-quality, publicly funded, *targeted* prekindergarten program for the poorest 25% of three- and four-year-old children would generate annual budgetary, earnings, and crime benefits that would surpass the annual costs of the program within six years. By the year 2050, the annual budgetary, earnings, and crime benefits would total $315 billion: $83 billion in government budget benefits, $156 billion in increased compensation of workers, and $77 billion in reduced costs to individuals of crime and child abuse. These annual benefits in 2050 would exceed the costs of the program in that year by a ratio of 12.1 to 1. Broken down by state, the total annual benefits would outstrip the annual costs of the program by a minimum of 8.1 to 1 for residents of Alabama and by as much as 29.1 to 1 for the residents of Delaware.

A high-quality, targeted pre-K program would cost nearly $6,300 per participant and could be expected to enroll just over 2 million children when it is fully phased in. Thus, the targeted program would initially cost taxpayers about $13.2 billion a year or, with offsets for current commitments to prekindergarten for at-risk children, an additional $8.2 billion per year once it is fully phased in. Such a program would ultimately reduce costs for remedial and special education, criminal justice, and child welfare, and would increase income earned and taxes paid. Within nine years, the net annual effect on government budgets would turn positive (for all levels of government combined). That is, starting the ninth year and every year thereafter, annual government budget benefits due to the program would outweigh annual government costs of the program. Within 44 years, the offsetting budget benefits alone would total $83 billion, more than three times the cost of the program. Thus by 2050, every tax dollar spent on the program would be offset by $3.18 in budget savings and governments collectively would be experiencing $57 billion in surpluses due to the pre-K investment.

Even if states covered the costs of the targeted program, with the federal government simply maintaining its current commitments to prekindergarten, the program would be a boon to state budgets. On average, states would experience net budget savings within 10 years, and by 2050, every dollar spent on the program would be offset by $2.15 in budgetary savings for state governments. These net budget savings would start within as few as four years in Delaware and in no more than 29 years in Alabama. By 2050, every state dollar expended on the program would be offset by at least $1.17 in budgetary savings for Alabama and as much as $4.97 in budget savings in Delaware. And in 2050, the federal government would be experiencing $29 billion in prekindergarten-related budget surplus. Whether funded by states or all levels of government, on top of the budget savings, by the year 2050, a targeted program is estimated to increase the compensation of workers by $156 billion and reduce the costs to individuals from crime and child abuse by $77 billion.

A voluntary, high-quality, publicly funded, *universal* prekindergarten program for all three- and four-year-olds would produce even greater annual budgetary, earnings, and crime benefits than would a targeted program. The annual benefits of the program would begin to outstrip its annual costs within nine years and would do so by a growing margin every year thereafter. By the year 2050, the annual benefits would total $779 billion: $191 billion in government budget benefits, $432 billion in increased compensation of workers, and $156 billion in reduced costs to individuals from less crime and child abuse. These annual benefits would exceed the costs of the program in 2050 by a ratio of 8.2 to 1. Broken down by state, in 2050 the total annual benefits would outstrip the annual costs of the program by a minimum of 6.1 to 1 for residents of Alabama and by as much as 11.4 to 1 for the residents of Wyoming.

A high-quality, publicly funded, *universal* prekindergarten program would cost nearly $6,300 per participant and could be expected to enroll almost 7 million children when it is fully phased in. Thus, the program would initially cost taxpayers $43.2 billion or, with offsets for current prekindergarten commitments, an additional $33.3 billion per annum once it is fully phased in. Within 17 years, the net annual effect on government budgets alone would turn positive, and by 2050 the budget savings would be $191 billion, double the total costs of the program in that year. Thus, in 2050, every tax dollar spent on a universal program would be offset by $2.00 in budget savings and governments would be enjoying $96 billion in surpluses as a consequence of their pre-K investment.

If the federal government refused to pay for any of the costs of the universal program and only maintained its current prekindergarten commitments, the program would generate budget surpluses in 46 states by 2050. Collectively, states would experience net budget savings with an average budget savings per state tax dollar spent on pre-K of $1.26 in 2050. The returns per state tax dollar spent would vary by state from a low of 79 cents in Alabama to a high of $1.88 in New York. The federal government would be enjoying $73 billion in prekindergarten investment related budget surplus in 2050.

Regardless of which level of government funds the program, in addition to the budget savings, by the year 2050, a universal program is estimated to increase the compensation of workers by $432 billion and reduce the costs to individuals of crime and child abuse by $156 billion.

A case for public investment in either a targeted or a universal prekindergarten program can be made with the best policy depending in part on whether a higher value is placed on the ratio of benefits to costs (which are higher for a targeted program) or the total net benefits (which are higher for a universal program). However, when policy makers weigh the benefits of investment in a targeted versus a universal program, other criteria should be taken into consideration. For example, if public funds are limited, a targeted program may be more attractive as it is less expensive to implement. Likewise, if a large priority is placed on narrowing the achievement gap between children from low-income and upper-income families, then the targeted program may be more effective in achieving this goal. On the other hand, a universal program available to all children may garner greater public support and thus be more likely to achieve the high-quality necessary for optimal results. Also, children who are not eligible for a targeted program can benefit from high-quality pre-K, and targeted programs are likely to fail to reach many of the children they are designed to serve. A universal program not only benefits middle- and upper-income children but may also have larger effects than a targeted program for the most at-risk children.

The economic and social benefits from prekindergarten investment amount to much more than just improvements in public balance sheets. Investing in young children has positive implications for the current, future, and earlier generations of children. The current generation of children will benefit from higher earnings, higher material standards of living, and an enhanced quality of life. Future generations will benefit because they will be less likely to grow up in families living in poverty. And earlier generations of children, who are now working or in retirement, will benefit by being supported by higher earning workers who will be better able to financially sustain our public retirement benefit programs such as Medicaid, Medicare, and Social Security. The pending retirement of the baby-boom generation will put enormous pressure on the federal budget in coming decades as more retirees draw from these benefit programs, and investing in high-quality prekindergarten education will provide much-needed future budget relief. In other words, strengthening the economic and social conditions of our youth will simultaneously help provide lasting economic security to future generations, to us, and to our elderly.

Investing in young children is likely to have enormous positive effects on the U.S. economy by raising GDP, improving the skills of the workforce, reducing poverty, and strengthening U.S. global competitiveness. Crime rates and the heavy costs of criminality to society are likely to be substantially reduced, as well. Additionally, given that the positive impacts of prekindergarten may be larger for at-risk than for more advantaged children, a pre-K program, whether targeted or universal, may help to reduce achievement gaps between poor and non-poor children, ultimately reducing income inequality nationwide.

Clearly, no single public policy can bring about the rapid and simultaneous achievement of *all* of our development goals, but just as clearly, policies do matter. And at a time of sharp disagreement over solutions to the many social and economic problems we confront, we should take particular notice when a consensus emerges across the political spectrum that the policy of investing in early childhood development in general, and in high-quality prekindergarten in particular, has the ability to powerfully impact many of our development goals and positively influence the pace of the development process. Investing in high-quality early childhood education programs is an effective public policy strategy that produces a wide array of significant benefits for children, their families, and society as a whole (including its taxpayers).

Although investment in early childhood education has the ability to positively impact many socioeconomic development goals, such investment has a particularly potent and direct bearing on the well-being of children, the educational achievement and productivity of children and adults, and crime. All three of these are areas where we have not only failed to achieve our potential, but also fallen short relative to other economically advanced nations. The United States should be investing now in high-quality prekindergarten to improve the quality of life of millions of American children, to make the workforce of the future more productive, to strengthen the economy, and to reduce crime. If the ultimate aim of public policy is to promote the wealth of nations, communities, families, and individuals, then investment in early childhood education is clearly a most effective strategy.

APPENDIX A

Omitted costs and benefits of targeted and universal prekindergarten

The ultimate costs and benefits of a large-scale, nationwide prekindergarten program enrolling 2 million children a year in a targeted program or nearly 7 million children per year in a universal program could turn out to be higher or lower than what we have estimated. For illustration purposes, this analysis assumes the launch of a targeted or a universal pre-K program on a national scale immediately in 2007, with full phase-in by 2008. But, for practical purposes, such as the recruitment and training of teachers and staff and the finding of appropriate locations, a large-scale pre-K program would have to be phased in over a longer period. There may be start-up costs associated with the scaling up of pre-K investment that have not been considered. Likewise, the quality of teachers and other staff may not be as good or as highly motivated as those in the Chicago CPC program may be.

On the other hand, the total benefits of prekindergarten investment are understated in our estimates and the omitted benefits surely outweigh any omitted costs. For example, we have not measured the financial savings to families who place their children in the publicly funded program but whom, in its absence, would have paid the costs of private preschool. Since about one-quarter of all families with three- and four-year-old children place their children in private preschool programs, the savings to families from the use of publicly funded prekindergarten are potentially very large, especially for a universal program. For example, if the average private program costs only half what the universal, publicly funded program costs and only 60% of children in private programs moved to the universal, high-quality, public program, then families who moved their children into the publicly funded prekindergarten program would save nearly $4 billion annually.

A large, nationwide, targeted prekindergarten program would have the potential not possible in small programs to improve the school atmosphere for everyone, not just pre-K participants. Raising the academic performance while lowering the drug and criminal activity of the 25% of children who attend high-quality targeted prekindergarten should benefit the other 75% of children who subsequently attend kindergarten through high school with them. This peer effect may be even greater for a universal program. If all children attend a high-quality pre-K program, the reductions in crime and school failure and the boosts to employment and earnings may be reinforcing and could produce much larger prekindergarten effects than those we have estimated in our analysis. Consequently, there may be some multiplier effects on the economy from the higher skilled, more productive, and higher earning universal pre-K participants.

There is also some evidence that a universal program may increase the effectiveness of prekindergarten education to the extent that a universal program integrates children from different economic backgrounds more thoroughly than a targeted program could. Schecter (2002) found that low-income children in economically integrated preschools fared better than comparable children in targeted programs that served only low-income children.

Perhaps most important in terms of omitted benefits, we do not calculate the potentially positive effects on the children born to pre-K participants who (as parents) will have higher earnings and employment and lower incarceration rates. Prekindergarten is an investment in the parents of the future who, because of pre-K education, will be able to provide better educational opportunities to their children than they would have without the pre-K program. Hence, the children of prekindergarten participants may be able to earn more and lead better lives. If this generational effect were properly accounted for, the benefits of pre-K education may be substantially larger than those we have estimated in this study.

We have also underestimated current government expenditures on state prekindergarten programs, Head Start, and special education by largely leaving out local government expenditures on these programs. Thus, the *additional* government outlays that we have estimated will be needed to fund our high-quality pre-K programs have been overstated. Other savings to taxpayers and boons to government budgets, such as reductions in public health care expenditures, may result from both targeted and universal prekindergarten, but these benefits were not calculated either. For example, there is some evidence that high-quality pre-K programs may reduce smoking (Schweinhart et al. 2005). This outcome, in turn, may reduce use of public health services.

Benefits were further underestimated as we limited ourselves to benefits for which it was possible to obtain monetary estimates. Thus, we left out benefits such as the intrinsic value of lower drug use, the value of fewer teenage parents, and the value of greater self-sufficiency when participants become adults.

Similarly, but perhaps more importantly, we omitted the value of the increase in the knowledge, skills, and literacy of students, the greater levels of happiness and job satisfaction of pre-K participants, and some of the value of the future greater productivity of more educated workers. To illustrate how large these omitted benefits may be, consider that between 1973 and 2004 average compensation in the United States increased 46% while average productivity increased 76% (Mishel, Bernstein, and Allegretto 2006). Thus, it is possible that the increase in compensation that we estimate will occur due to prekindergarten investment reflects only about two-thirds of the increase in productivity that will take place in the economy. This implies that our estimates of the benefits of the targeted and universal programs in the year 2050 are missing over $75 billion and $215 billion, respectively, in productivity increases. If future increases in productivity due to pre-K investment are not fully captured in our estimated compensation gains, then we are omitting a very large benefit of prekindergarten since these productivity increases will manifest themselves in some other form such as in increases in profits.

There is at least one set of costs and reductions to benefits that we have appropriately included in the costs and benefits of the targeted program but, perhaps, should have excluded from the costs and benefits of the universal program. Thus, relative to the targeted program, the costs of the universal program may be somewhat overstated and its benefits estimates may be somewhat understated.

In particular, in a targeted program where the enrolment eligibility is based in part on the income of children's families, a mechanism must be put in place to screen children for income eligibility. Such a mechanism will cost money, will be imperfect, and is unnecessary in a universal program. The consequence is that there will be some additional cost to a targeted program relative to a universal program. In addition, given that the screening mechanism is unlikely to be perfect, allowing some non-poor children to enroll in the targeted program, the benefits of a targeted program may be reduced as a result of the participation of some less at-risk children.

It is costly to ensure that all income-eligible children participate and all income-ineligible children are excluded from a targeted program (Barnett, Brown, and Shore 2004). The eligible population will be difficult to identify because it will constantly change as national and family economic conditions vary. Some poor families will not enroll their children, as they will be unaware that they are eligible. The income eligibility of children may have to be re-analyzed as their families move from one school district to another. Some ineligible children will be enrolled because mistakes will be made in the screening process and some families will work the system by hiding their true income. These ineligible and perhaps less at-risk children may experience lower benefits from a targeted program than would the eligible children. Given that we have appropriately included these increased costs and lower benefits in our estimates of the costs and benefits of the targeted program but failed to exclude them from the costs and benefits of the universal program, the costs of the universal program may be somewhat overstated and its benefits estimates may be somewhat understated.

We also left out the value of other likely, but difficult to quantify, benefits of prekindergarten. For example, given the correlation between education attainment and voting, we failed to include the value of the greater involvement of citizens in the democratic process that is likely to result from pre-K participation. In total, the value of the omitted benefits are likely to swamp the value of the omitted costs, and the total benefits and the benefit-cost ratios of both the targeted and the universal programs are likely to be much larger than those we have presented in this book.

Sensitivity analysis for targeted and universal prekindergarten

As noted in our discussion of some of the difficulties in estimating the costs and benefits of a universal program, it is not certain how much the impacts of high-quality prekindergarten (whether targeted or universal) should be attenuated to account for the fact that some of the children who would attend such a program, in its absence, would have received some of its benefits by attending some other preschool program. In our estimates of the impacts of targeted and universal pre-K, we assumed that participants who would have attended some other preschool program in the absence of the high-quality public program would experience only 60% of the impacts experienced by the Chicago CPC participants. In other words, the attenuation of high-quality pre-K effectiveness to account for current preschool enrollment is assumed to be 40%. In the sensitivity analysis below, we allow this attenuation to vary from as much as 70% to as little as 10%.

In the targeted program, when we assumed 40% attenuation to account for the effects of current preschool enrollment rates, we estimated that prekindergarten investment would generate a net government budgetary surplus of $57 billion per year in 2050 and every dollar spent in 2050 would be offset by $3.18 in budget savings in that year. The increase in compensation was estimated to amount to $156 billion and the savings to individuals from less crime was $77 billion in 2050. With attenuation due to current preschool enrollment allowed to vary from as much as 70% to as little as 10%, the budgetary surplus would range from $45 billion to $68 billion per year in 2050, the return per tax dollar invested in 2050 would vary from $2.83 to $3.51, the increase in compensation would be between $132 billion and $179 billion per year in 2050, and the savings to individuals from less crime would vary from $65 billion to $89 billion per year in the year 2050.

Aside from various attenuation rates for current preschool enrollment, in a sensitivity analysis of the *universal* program we must consider that a large-scale universal pre-K program would draw in more children from middle- and upper-income families who are at lower risk for educational failure and other problems than those in the targeted program. Such kids might (or might not) experience smaller positive impacts from prekindergarten than those in the targeted program. In our estimate of the costs and benefits of a universal program, we assumed that middle-income and upper-income children would experience 85% and 70%, respectively, of the impacts of prekindergarten experienced by lower income children. These and the following estimates of the impact of high-quality pre-K were then adjusted to account for the different levels of social and academic problems experienced by children from families with different incomes. In the sensitivity analysis below, we examine the costs and benefits of universal pre-K when we both vary attenuation rates for current preschool enrollment and allow middle- and upper-income children to experience as much as 100% and as little as 70% and 40%, respectively, of the high-quality pre-K effects experienced by low-income children.[41]

Our most conservative or lowest estimate of the effects of universal pre-K assumes attenuation due to current preschool enrollment of 70% and pre-K impacts on middle- and uppe-income children that are only 70% and 40%, respectively, of those for the Chicago CPC participants. Our highest estimate of the effects of universal pre-K assumes attenuation due to current preschool enrollment of 10% and pre-K impacts on middle- and upper-income children that are 100% of those for the Chicago CPC participants.[42]

Our lowest and highest estimates of the effects of universal pre-K investment suggest that this investment would, in 2050, generate a budgetary surplus of at least $45 billion and as much as $156 billion, a return per tax dollar invested of at least $1.50 and as much as $2.51, an increase in compensation of between $301 billion and $588 billion, and savings to individuals from less crime and child abuse that vary from a low of $109 billion to a high of $210 billion.

In other words, even adjusting for a very wide range of estimates for the effects of current preschool participation and the impact of high-quality prekindergarten education on children from different economic backgrounds, high-quality universal pre-K has substantial long-run benefits for government budgets, the economy, and crime reduction. Pre-K participants, their families, and society all benefit from publicly financed prekindergarten. Although the government budget benefit-cost ratio of a national scale prekindergarten program (whether targeted or universal) could be somewhat higher or lower than the preferred estimate presented in this paper, it is improbable that this ratio would be less than the 1-to-1 ratio necessary for the program to eventually pay for itself.

APPENDIX B

Explanation of the methodology for estimating the budget, earnings, and crime effects of investments in prekindergarten

The methodology used to calculate the costs, benefits, and enrollment rates in targeted and universal prekindergarten, the attenuation of pre-K effects for middle- and upper-income children and for prior preschool attendance, and the projection process are explained in more detail below. We begin with a description of government costs and savings and then move to a description of the calculations for private savings. Next, the estimated attenuation of prekindergarten effects for middle- and upper- income children, the accounting for prior preschool attendance, and the enrollment rate estimates are described. Finally, the process of accruing costs and benefits through time is explained.[43]

Government costs and savings

Cost of proposed prekindergarten program

Reynolds et al. (2002) create a cost estimate for the Chicago Child-Parent Center (CPC) program of $4,400 in 1998 dollars by inflating a 1986 estimate of the program's cost using the CPI-U.[44] We were concerned that this method would lead to an understatement of the true cost of the program, as growth in the cost of early childhood education outpaced CPI-U inflation over the period. An inflation series that more accurately reflects the growth in costs of early childhood education, a CPI series covering Child Care and Nursery Schools (CCNS), is available beginning in 1990. Thus, the Reynolds et al. (2002) estimate was deflated back to 1990 using their own inflators, then inflated from 1990 to 2005 using CCNS. From 2005 to 2050, the costs of the pre-K program were inflated 3.5% annually, in line with projections by CBO (2004) for inflation of 2.2% and real earnings growth of 1.3%. We reasoned that the production of education services is more labor intensive than the production of most other goods and services. Thus, adjusting education costs by inflation alone was likely to understate the true growth of the costs of providing education services given that nominal earnings growth was expected by CBO to exceed inflation.

This program cost was then varied by state assuming that state-by-state variation is due largely to differences in teacher salaries across states and that other costs are fairly similar across states. The portion of the program cost attributed to instructional staff per Reynolds et al. (2002) was varied with a state teacher pay index constructed using average teacher pay by state calculated from the 2000 decennial Census data. Because the original program was in Chicago, Illinois was used as the base for the index.

Program cost offsets

Given that the proposed high-quality prekindergarten education program would be a substitute for some of the existing public pre-K programs, a portion of current spending on state public pre-K, equal to the share of public pre-K participants who would be attending the proposed high-quality programs, was subtracted, by state, from the program costs so as to not double count these expenditures. Enrollment in and expenditures on existing public pre-K programs was taken from the *The State of Preschool 2005* published by the National Institute for Early Education Reseach (NIEER) (Barnett et al. 2005b). In addition, given that the high-quality prospective pre-K program would attract children who in its absence would otherwise enroll in Head Start, a portion of the Head Start expenditures (Barnett et al. 2005b) equal to the amount spent on a half-day of Head Start per proposed prekindergarten participant who would otherwise have attended Head Start was subtracted, by state, from the program costs to ensure that expenditures were not double counted. The amount spent on a half-day of Head Start was estimated by dividing the total Head Start expenditures by state by one plus the proportion of children enrolled full-day, five days a week in Head Start by state as reported by NIEER (Barnett et al. 2005b). The federal government and states currently allocate funds for special education programs for three- and four-year-olds. Some three- and four-year-olds who require special education services will enroll in the proposed prekindergarten program and we assumed that special education expenditures will continue to fund programs for these children. Specifically, for each prospective pre-K participant who would require special education services we apportioned two-thirds of current special education expenditures per recipient, by state (Parrish et al. 2004), to the funding of the proposed pre-K programs: we assumed that this represented roughly 100% of special education monies spent on children who get half-day or less of special education services and 50% of special education monies spent on children who get more than a half-day of special education services.

Cost of increased high school usage

Reynolds et al. (2002) found that Chicago CPC participants completed one-third of a year more of public education than did non-participants. Obviously, this imposes a cost on governments who must pay for the additional time spent by pre-K participants in public education.

State-by-state estimates of per-pupil expenditures on public K-12 education in 2004-05 (Hovey and Hovey 2006) were inflated to 2006 dollars using CBO's (June

2004) estimate of nominal wage inflation. We felt it was reasonable to use CBO's estimate of nominal wage inflation (3.5%), which is higher than its estimate for average price increases (2.2%), as education costs have been rising faster than average prices for some time. Costs are divided between the federal government and state and local governments using state-by-state estimates of the federal share of K-12 public school revenue (State Policy Reports 2006). The annual costs of high school were then multiplied by the extra amount of time spent in high school due to the effects of the Chicago CPC program as calculated by Reynolds et al. (2002, 279, Table 4). These costs are realized when a student reaches age 17.

Costs of increased higher education

Chicago CPC participants had a high school graduation rate that was 11.2% higher than it was for the control group. Many of these high school graduates went on to attend public institutions of higher education that are subsidized by governments.

State-by-state estimates of state and local appropriations for higher education are available for fiscal year 2004 (Center for the Study of Education Policy 2006, Grapevine Table 9,), while state-by-state data on the distribution of total federal higher education appropriations, grants, and contracts are available only through 2002 (Digest of Education Statistics 2004). To correct for this mismatch, total federal higher education appropriations for fiscal year 2004 were distributed by state according to the available 2002 state-by-state data.

In order to calculate the per-student spending in fiscal year 2004, the total federal, state, and local higher education spending calculated above must be divided by total higher education enrollment. Total higher education enrollment for that year was obtained from the National Center for Education Statistics (U.S. Department of Education 2005). But, as with federal grants and appropriations, the state-by-state enrollment data are available only through 2002. Following the procedure described above to distribute federal appropriations, the 2004 enrollment was distributed by states in the same pattern as the 2002 enrollment data.

These 2004 figures were inflated to 2005 dollars using the Bureau of Labor Statistics CPI series covering college tuition and fees (CT&F), then to 2006 dollars using CBO's (2004) estimate of nominal wage inflation.

Both the federal and state appropriations were divided by enrollment, giving the average per-student per-year cost of higher education. This figure was then multiplied by the average years in college for high school graduates (U.S. Census Bureau, PINC-04, 2004b), and the high school graduation treatment effect of the CPC program, yielding estimates of the per participant cost to both the state and federal governments of increased higher education usage by prekindergarten program participants. This per participant cost was spread over a five-year period assuming that people complete their college experience over a five-year time frame from age 18 to 22, as assumed by Reynolds et al. (2002).

The costs of the additional higher education expenditures due to the effect of the prekindergarten program were apportioned between federal and state governments in proportion to their expenditures on higher education.

Savings from reduced special education

Children who participated in the Chicago CPC program spent an average of 0.7 fewer years in special education than did children in the comparison group. An estimate of the average per-year per-student cost of special education in 2000 (Parrish et al. 2004) was inflated to 2005 dollars using the CPI series elementary and high school tuition and fees (E&HS), then to 2006 dollars using CBO's (2004) estimate of wage inflation. This cost estimate was multiplied by the CPC treatment effect on years spent in special education yielding the per-participant savings due to decreased use of special education. The per-participant savings due to decreased use of special education was weighted to take into account the actual family income distribution of participants within the prospective pre-K program. These savings were then divided between the state and federal governments using state-by-state estimates of the federal share of special education spending (Parrish et al. 2004). Total savings were spread over 13 years to arrive at the yearly savings from kindergarten through 12th grade as a result of less special education usage.

Savings from less grade retention

Children who participated in the Chicago CPC program were retained in grade 15.4% less often than the comparison group. The per-student per-year cost of K-12 education calculated above was multiplied by the average reduction in grade repetition for CPC participants, expressed in years (assuming that children were retained in grade for only one year), yielding the average per-participant reduction in expenditures on additional schooling related to grade retention. For the targeted program, this savings was then multiplied by a factor reflecting the larger baseline probability that children in the lowest income quartile will repeat a grade (Karoly and Bigelow 2005). For the universal program, this savings was multiplied by a factor reflecting the larger baseline probability that children in the lowest quartile will repeat a grade and by a factor reflecting the smaller probability that children not in the lowest income quartile will repeat a grade, weighted to reflect the family income distribution of the students in the prospective universal prekindergarten program.

The savings from less grade retention were then divided between federal and state governments according to their shares of the total spending on K-12 education, and spread over the 13-year period from age five to age 17.

Child welfare savings from decreased child maltreatment

Children who participated in the Chicago CPC program were 51% less likely to be victims of child abuse or neglect. This reduction in child maltreatment generates savings in child welfare.

Child maltreatment investigations can lead to two findings: that a child is a victim of maltreatment, or that the child is a non-victim. The finding that a child is a non-victim does not necessarily preclude further action, but action such as removal from the home is far less frequent in the case of non-victims. Thus, these two populations are treated separately in the following savings calculations.

The total number of victims and the total number of non-victims in 2000 (U.S. Department of Health and Human Services 2004) were each divided by the total child population in the same year to determine the proportion of children ruled to be victims or non-victims of child maltreatment.

The total cost of foster care in the year 2000 (Bees et al. 2003) was divided by the total number of foster care recipients in that year (U.S. Department of Health and Human Services 2005a), yielding the per-recipient, per-year cost of foster care. The proportions of victims and non-victims removed from the home (U.S. Department of Health and Human Services 2004) were multiplied by the proportions of the child population (state-by-state) ruled to be victims or non-victims respectively, and these products were summed, yielding the proportion of the total child population removed from the home. This proportion was then multiplied by the average years spent in foster care by children removed from the home (U.S. Department of Health and Human Services 2005c), and the previously calculated per-recipient per-year cost of foster care, yielding the per-year per-*child* cost of foster care for a given population. This cost was multiplied by the reduction in the likelihood that a child would be the victim of maltreatment as a consequence of participation in the CPC program (CPC child welfare treatment effect), yielding per-recipient government savings from reduced foster care use. This savings was then inflated from 2000 dollars to 2006 dollars using the CPI-U.

Foster care recipients receive adoption services. The total cost of adoption services in 2000 (Bees et al. 2003) was divided by the total number of foster care recipients in that year, yielding the per-recipient per-year cost of adoption services. This cost was then multiplied by the average number of years a recipient receives adoption services (U.S. Department of Health and Human Services 2005c), and the CPC child welfare treatment effect, yielding the per-participant adoption services savings. This savings estimate was then inflated from 2000 dollars to 2006 dollars using the CPI-U.

The savings due to other post-investigative services were calculated by multiplying the proportions of victims and non-victims receiving these services (U.S. Department of Health and Human Services 2004) by the proportion of the children who were victims and non-victims respectively (all state-by-state), summing these products and multiplying the results by the per-case cost of these additional services (Courtney 1998) and the CPC child welfare treatment effect. This per-participant post-investigative services saving was then inflated from 1993 dollars to 2006 dollars using CPI-U.

Child maltreatment investigations are costly in themselves. The per-child rate of investigations was calculated by dividing the total number of investigations (U.S. Department of Health and Human Services, 2004) by the total child population (both state-by-state). This rate was then multiplied by the per-case cost of investigations (Courtney 1998), and the CPC child welfare treatment effect, yielding the per-participant savings in child maltreatment investigations. These savings were then inflated from 1993 dollars to 2006 dollars using the CPI-U.

Finally, there are significant governmental costs associated with child maltreatment that are not reflected in the above figures. This residual was calculated by subtracting total expenditures on the above items from an estimate of total expenditures on child welfare services (Bees et al. 2003). This figure was then divided by the total child population, multiplied by the CPC child welfare treatment effect, and inflated from 2000 to 2006 using the CPI-U, yielding the per-participant savings in otherwise uncategorized child welfare spending.

The per participant savings in foster care, adoption services, investigations, post-investigative services, and residual welfare spending were then summed. Children in families whose income is in the bottom quartile of the income distribution account for a disproportionate share of child maltreatment cases. Data from Sedlak and Broadhurst (1996) suggest that children in the poorest quarter of families account for approximately 57% of cases of child maltreatment. For the targeted prekindergarten program, the average per participant savings were multiplied by a factor reflecting the greater overall usage of child welfare services by children in the bottom quartile of the family income distribution. For the universal program, the average per participant savings were multiplied by a factor reflecting the greater overall usage of child welfare services by children in the bottom quartile of the family income distribution and by a factor reflecting the lower overall usage of child welfare services by children not in the bottom quartile of the family income distribution, weighted to take into account the actual income distribution within the prospective universal program.

The resulting per-participant savings was adjusted to factor out savings that could only occur in the first three years of life: the years before a child could attend prekindergarten and experience any pre-K induced reduction in maltreatment. The resulting adjusted per-participant savings from less maltreatment was divided between the state and federal governments using state-by-state data on the federal share of child welfare spending (Bees et al. 2003), and spread over the 15 years from age three to age 17.

Savings from reduced juvenile crime

Children who participated in the Chicago CPC program were 42% less likely to be arrested by age 18 than were the children in the comparison group. This prekindergarten effect generates substantial potential savings in criminal justice system costs.

Arrest costs are higher for violent crime than non-violent crime. The total per-child cost of juvenile arrests was calculated by multiplying state-by-state violent and non-violent juvenile arrest rates (Snyder et al. 2005) by per-arrest costs of violent and non-violent juvenile arrests (Aos et al. 2001), and summing these products.

Most juvenile arrests are dealt with in juvenile court, but some are waived to adult court. The cost of cases handled in juvenile court is calculated by multiplying the per-arrest cost of adjudication (Aos et al. 2001) by the number of arrests adjudicated delinquent (Snyder et al. 2005), adding the product of the per-incarceration cost of incarceration (Aos et al. 2001) and the number of juvenile arrests leading to incarceration (Stahl et al. 2005), the product of the average cost of juvenile probation (Aos et al. 2001) and the number of juvenile arrests leading to probation (Stahl et al. 2005), and the product of the average cost of juvenile detention (Miller et al. 2001), and the number of juvenile arrests leading to detention (Stahl et al. 2005), then dividing this sum by the total number of juvenile arrests dealt with in juvenile court (Snyder et al. 2005), yielding the per-arrest cost of juvenile court adjudication and punishment.

Adult court adjudication of juveniles is somewhat more costly than juvenile court adjudication of juveniles. However, in calculating the crime costs of juveniles who were adjudicated in adult courts we used the lower cost estimates for juvenile court adjudication because the full costs and outcomes of adult court adjudication of juveniles were not available. Thus, the per-arrest cost of adult court adjudication and punishment in juvenile cases was calculated in the same fashion as juvenile court adjudications, but multiplied by the number of juvenile arrests handled in adult court weighted by the juvenile court rate of convictions per arrest, incarcerations per arrest, and probations per arrest (Stahl et al. 2005). The major difference between the two types of adjudication is the addition of parole costs (Aos et al. 2001) to adult court adjudication.

The per-arrest cost of juvenile and adult court adjudication and punishment are each expressed in terms of total juvenile arrests, and are thus summed to create the total per-arrest cost of adjudication and punishment of juvenile crime. This sum was multiplied by state-by-state juvenile arrest rates (Snyder et al. 2005), yielding the per-*child* cost of juvenile adjudication and punishment, which was added to the previously calculated per-child cost of juvenile arrests to arrive at the total per-child cost of juvenile crime.

We assumed children commit crimes over an eight-year period between the ages of 10 and 17. Hence, the per-child cost of juvenile crime was multiplied by 18 and divided by eight to arrive at the per-juvenile cost of juvenile crime.

Our estimate of total per-juvenile cost of juvenile crime is perhaps lower than the true total per-juvenile cost of juvenile crime. Based on the ratio of juvenile arrests to total arrests, Levitt and Lochner (2002) estimate that between 20% and 30% of total justice system expenditures are for juvenile crime. Applying Levitt and Lochner's estimate suggests that spending on juvenile crime by the justice system in 2000 amounted to between $31 billion and $47 billion. By contrast, our estimate of total spending on juvenile crime by the justice system amounts to just over $18 billion in 2000. If the justice system costs associated with dealing with juvenile crime are lower than costs associated with dealing with adult crime (e.g., shorter and less expensive trials, shorter periods of incarceration, etc.), then our estimate may be more accurate than Levitt and Lochner's.

The total cost per-juvenile of juvenile crime was then inflated to 2006 dollars using the CPI-U and multiplied by the CPC juvenile crime treatment effect. Juveniles in poverty have a higher propensity to commit crime and engage in criminal behavior. For example, data from Mocan and Rees (1999) suggest that juveniles in families on welfare account for a disproportionate share of juvenile crime. Hence, for the targeted prekindergarten program our estimate of juvenile crime savings was multiplied by a factor reflecting the greater overall criminal justice costs for children in the bottom quartile of the family income distribution (Mocan and Rees 1999, 7). For the universal prekindergarten program, our estimate of juvenile crime savings was multiplied by a factor reflecting the greater overall criminal justice costs for children in the bottom quartile of the family income distribution and by a factor reflecting the lower overall criminal justice costs for children not in the bottom quartile of the family income distribution, weighted to take into account the actual income distribution within the prospective universal program.

The savings in juvenile criminal justice system costs were apportioned between federal and state governments based on their shares of total spending on criminal justice in 2000 (U.S. Bureau of Justice 2006), and spread over the eight year period from age 10 through age 17.

Savings from reduced adult crime

One of the best predictors of an adult's involvement in criminal activity is their crime record as a juvenile. Reductions in juvenile crime due to prekindergarten participation are, thus, likely to result in reductions in adult crime.

The detailed cost estimates available for juvenile crime in the area of judicial proceedings (courts), corrections, and policing are unfortunately not available for adult crime, so the calculus used to arrive at adult crime savings is somewhat different from that used to generate juvenile crime savings.

First, an estimate of total per-year expenditures on juvenile judicial proceedings and corrections was created by multiplying the previously calculated per-child expenditures on juvenile judicial proceedings and corrections (excluding arrest costs, which were dealt with separately) by the child population in that year. This juvenile expenditures estimate was subtracted from an estimate of total per-year expenditures on judicial proceedings and corrections, yielding total per-year expenditures on *adult* judicial proceedings and corrections.

Determining the total expenditures on policing related to adult crime is somewhat more complicated. While there are certainly estimates of total expenditures on policing, these estimates do not differentiate between policing costs directly related to criminal arrests and all other policing costs such as those related to facilitating traffic flow or providing security at parades. The CPC treatment effect is a reduction in arrests, which would not affect, say, expenditures on traffic enforcement. An estimate of total policing expenditures on crime was created assuming that the ratio of juvenile crime-related policing costs to adult crime-related policing costs is equal to the ratio of juvenile crime-related judicial proceedings and corrections to adult crime-related judicial proceedings and corrections. The previously calculated per-child per-year cost of juvenile arrests was multiplied by the child population, yielding the total per-year cost of juvenile arrests, which was then scaled up using the ratio of adult judicial and correctional expenditures to juvenile judicial and correctional expenditures. This gave an estimate of total per-year adult crime-related policing expenses. As expected, the sum of juvenile crime-related policing expenditures and adult crime-related policing expenditures amounted to substantially less than total justice system expenditures on policing (e.g., $45 billion versus $69 billion in 2000), allowing for expenditures on non-crime related policing.

The per-year adult policing expenses were added to the per-year adult judicial and correctional expenditures, yielding the total per-year cost of adult crime. This was divided by the total adult population between the ages of 18 and 44, yielding the average per-year per-adult cost of adult crime, which was then inflated from 2000 dollars to 2006 dollars using the CPI-U and distributed by state based on state arrest rates (Snyder et al. 2005). The savings in adult criminal justice system costs were apportioned between federal and state governments based on their shares of total spending on criminal justice in 2000 (U.S. Bureau of Justice 2006), and spread over the 27-year period between age 18 and age 44 as described in a later section.

Savings from greater taxes and earnings due to increased labor force participation made possible by publicly funded prekindergarten

A publicly funded prekindergarten program will effectively provide parents of three- and four-year-old children with free child care for the time that the children are in pre-K. As a result, parents of participating children will be more likely to enter the labor market, secure a position, earn greater income, and pay more in taxes.

The average work year is approximately 2,000 hours, and average commuting hours are about 192 hours per year (Bartik 2001). The prospective pre-K program lasts 525 hours per year and thus provides approximately a 25% child care subsidy for each of two years.

Many of the prospective universal and targeted pre-K participants, in the absence of these proposed programs, would attend some other form of public preschool and get this child care subsidy. However, in the presence of the proposed prekindergarten programs, the child care subsidy would be extended to parents who would switch their children from private preschool or private child care to public prekindergarten and to parents who would enroll their children in the public program who otherwise would have enrolled them in no child care program. Thus, we reduce the per prekindergarten participant child care subsidy by a factor that reflects the percent of participants who, in the absence of a public high-quality program, would otherwise have had publicly financed child care to estimate an effective subsidy rate.

Research suggests that the percentage point increase in labor force participation for a given reduction in child care costs is about 0.2 or more (Bartik 2006; Blau 2001; Blau and Hagy 1998; Anderson and Levine 2000). There is data to suggest that this elasticity measure is greater than 0.2 for mothers with children under the age of six, but to arrive at a conservative estimate of the employment effect of subsidized child care, we use the lower 0.2 elasticity measure.

The effective subsidy rate is multiplied by the 0.2 elasticity measure and the number of pre-K participants to get a rough estimate of the increase in the labor force participation rate as a result of the publicly funded pre-K program. Assuming little or no displacement in the job market, this increase in labor force participation translates into new jobs created.

The new jobs created by the targeted prekindergarten program are multiplied by the 20th percentile of wages to arrive at an estimate of the increase in earnings due to the targeted program. The new jobs created by the universal prekindergarten program are multiplied by the 50th percentile of wages to arrive at an estimate of the increase in earnings due to the universal program. Earnings were multiplied by 1.25 to include non-wage compensation and arrive at an estimate of the increase in total compensation for the guardians of pre-K participants.

The increase in earnings due to the targeted program, calculated above, are multiplied by an estimate of the average federal state and local tax rate (by state) that applies to the lowest quintile of income earners (Institute for Taxation and Economic Policy 2003). The increase in earnings due to the universal program, calculated above, are multiplied by an estimate of the average federal state and local tax rate (by state) that applies to the middle quintile of income earners (ITEP 2003).

Compensation, earnings, and taxes due to greater educational attainment of prekindergarten participants

The 11.2% increase in the high school graduation rate of Chicago CPC participants can be used to predict the future increases in compensation, earnings, and taxes associated with prekindergarten participation. From Census data (U.S. Census Bureau 2004d), we took the mean earnings for all people under age 65 for the categories "less than ninth grade," " ninth to 12th nongrad," "high school including GED," "some college no degree," "associate degree," and "college degree total." We calculated the weighted average earnings for those without a high school degree in 2004 and subtracted it from the weighted average earnings of those with a high school degree or greater in 2004.[45] We multiplied the estimated earnings differential by the high-quality prekindergarten effect for greater high school graduation, per Reynolds et al. (2002) to estimate the average increase in earnings per prospective pre-K participant in 2004 dollars. The average increase in earnings per prospective pre-K participant were inflated by CPI-U "Total Private Average Earnings: Hourly Earnings of Production Workers" to 2005 then to 2006 dollars using CBO's (June 2004) estimate of nominal wage inflation. Earnings were multiplied by 1.25 to include non-wage compensation and then taxes were subtracted to estimate the after-tax earnings and compensation increase per prospective prekindergarten participant.

Taxes on the increased earnings were calculated by applying the federal, state, and local average tax rates (by state) for the middle quintile of earners in the case of the universal program and the lowest quintile of earners for the targeted program (ITEP 2003). State-by-state earnings were adjusted using an estimate of average annual pay variation by state.[46]

The projected gains in compensation, earnings, and taxes associated with prekindergarten participation may have been underestimated. Our approach to calculating these gains implicitly assumes that the earnings differentials due to schooling attainment that exist today will remain constant in the future. But returns to additional quantities of education have been increasing for the last several decades and this trend may continue in the future given the increasing relative demand for educated workers. In addition, our approach assumes that prekindergarten participants without a high school degree will earn no more than non-participants without a high school degree will earn, even though the pre-K participants are likely to experience a host of benefits from prekindergarten attendance, including greater educational attainment, lower involvement in crime, less child maltreatment, and less need for education related remedial services. Indeed, applying our approach to the Perry Preschool participants underestimates their actual earnings gains at ages 27 and 40 relative to the control group.

Private savings[47]

Reduced crime, child abuse, and neglect create benefits for society beyond those that accrue to government through reductions in criminal justice system costs and child welfare expenditures. The costs to victims of crime and child abuse and neglect can be divided into "tangible costs" and "intangible costs." Tangible costs are costs to victims such as property losses, medical care, lost productivity, and mental health care costs. Intangible costs are reductions in the well-being of victims, such as pain and suffering, which have been monetized so that they might be compared to other costs and benefits.

Tangible and intangible savings from reduced child abuse and neglect

The previously calculated proportion of children who will be the victim of child abuse or neglect was first multiplied by the proportion of victims who are abused and the proportion of victims who are neglected to arrive at the proportion of *children* who will be abused and the proportion of *children* who will be neglected. These proportions were each multiplied by estimates of both the tangible and intangible costs of the relevant type of victimization: child abuse is estimated to be significantly more costly than neglect (Miller et al. 1996). The tangible costs of abuse and the tangible costs of neglect were summed, yielding the tangible costs of child maltreatment. The intangible costs of abuse and neglect were also summed, yielding the intangible costs of child maltreatment.

These cost estimates were inflated from 1993 to 2006 via the CPI-U, and multiplied by the pre-K child maltreatment treatment effect (Reynolds et al. 2002), yielding the per-participant tangible and intangible savings from reduced abuse and neglect. For the targeted pre-K program, the average per-participant savings were multiplied by a factor reflecting the greater overall usage of child welfare services by children in the bottom quartile of the family income distribution. For the universal program, the average per-participant savings were multiplied by a factor reflecting the greater overall usage of child welfare services by children in the bottom quartile of the family income distribution and by a factor reflecting the lower overall usage of child welfare services by children not in the bottom quartile of the family income distribution, weighted to take into account the actual income distribution within the prospective universal program.

Tangible and intangible effects of crime

The societal effects of crime reduction, both tangible and intangible, are estimated to be 4.5 times the governmental savings in criminal justice system costs (Schweinhart et al. 1993). Hence, for both the targeted and universal prekindergarten program the juvenile and adult crime savings for criminal justice were multiplied by 4.5 to arrive at the tangible and intangible savings from less juvenile and adult crime.

Attenuation of prekindergarten effects for children from middle- and upper-income families

To calculate the effects of a universal program we must estimate the extent to which the benefits of a high-quality prekindergarten program like the Chicago CPC program, which served high-risk children (from low-income families), would apply to medium-risk children (from middle-income families) and low-risk children (from high-income families) who would otherwise attend no preschool. The Chicago CPC program and studies of other high-quality programs that targeted low-income children found significant long-run benefits for high-risk children, including greater academic achievement, lower rates of criminal activity, reduced child abuse and neglect, higher schooling attainment, and higher employment and earnings. However, these high-quality targeted programs did not include children from middle- and upper-income families and thus they do not provide evidence of the long-term effects of high-quality prekindergarten participation on more advantaged children. Unfortunately, there are not many studies that have examined the benefits of high-quality prekindergarten on middle- and low-risk children.

Differential pre-K benefits for children with different backgrounds manifest in two ways. First, there is a baseline effect: different populations have different rates of everything from child abuse to special education to criminal behavior. This different baseline can be thought of as a "room for improvement" effect. Secondly, there may be a differential treatment effect: for reasons not captured fully by the baseline differences, different children may see greater or lesser treatment effects from prekindergarten.

It is reasonable to expect that the benefits of high-quality prekindergarten will be more positive for less-advantaged children than they will be for more-advantaged children because there is more room for improvement among poor children. The incidence of academic and social problems is generally higher for high-risk children than it is for more-advantaged children.[48] For example, rates of grade retention are 18.2% for poor children, 13.1% for middle-income children, and 9.1% for upper-income children (Karoly and Bigelow 2005, 44). Thus, middle-income children have about 72% the rate of grade retention that poor children have and upper-income children are retained at about 50% of the rate of poor children. Similarly, the use of special education is about 16.8% among children from families in the lowest quarter of the income distribution, versus 11.3% among children from families in the middle half of the income distribution, and about 6.3% among children from families in the top quarter of the income distribution. In other words, children from middle-income and well-to-do families use special education at roughly 67% and 38%, respectively, the rate of low-income children (Karoly and Bigelow 2005, 46). Likewise, poor children are disproportionately involved in crime and are more likely to be victims of child abuse and neglect than are non-poor children. Similarly, a positive relationship between family income and school readiness was found in The Early Childhood Longitudinal Study: kindergarten class of 1998-99 (U.S. Department of Education 2006). The scores on tests of literacy, math skills, general knowledge, and social skills for children who entered kindergarten increased gradually with family income. The shortfalls in scores of poor children relative to middle-income children were similar to the shortfalls in the scores of middle-income children relative to upper-income children.[49]

Collectively, these data suggest that high-quality prekindergarten programs may be able to generate smaller benefits from low-risk kids than from high-risk kids. For example, if a high-quality pre-K program cuts subsequent juvenile crime rates by an equal proportion for all children, the savings in criminal justice costs per pre-K participant will be smaller for low-risk kids to the extent that they are less involved in crime than are high-risk kids. Assuming for illustration purposes that the average low-risk child commits two crimes while the average high-risk child commits four crimes and that the pre-K program cuts crime rates in half for all children, then the criminal justice system will be spared the costs of only one crime per low-risk child but a greater two crimes per high-risk child due to the pre-K program. This is the baseline effect: a lower starting point leaves more room for absolute improvement.

Aside from the fact that the room for improvement differs among children from various socio-economic backgrounds, the empirical research on the measured impacts of prekindergarten generally shows that lower-, middle-, and upper-income children benefit significantly from high-quality prekindergarten. However, the literature shows mixed findings on how much these groups of children benefit and on which of these groups of children benefits most.

Larsen and Robinson (1989) compared two groups of low-risk children from above-average income and educationally advantaged families: one that had been assigned to a prekindergarten and the other that did not attend prekindergarten locally (but members of which may have attended a preschool program out of the local area) and served as the control group. Among the girls, there were no statistically significant differences in outcomes, but the girls in the prekindergarten scored higher on nine of 11 achievement tests than the girls in the control group. The boys in the prekindergarten program scored higher on all 11 tests and significantly higher on reading vocabulary, total reading, spelling, total language, and the total battery than did the boys in the control group. The gains from attending prekindergarten for both boys and girls may have been greater had the control group been composed only of low-risk children who attended no other preschool.

Garces, Thomas, and Currie (2000), analyzing data for children born between 1964 and 1977, compared outcomes for high-risk children who attended Head Start to high-risk kids who attended no preschool. They also compared outcomes for lower risk children who attended preschool other than Head Start (mostly private preschools) to lower risk children who did not attend any preschool. They found that white high-risk children who attended Head Start had higher high school graduation rates and college attendance than did comparable whites who attended no preschool. In addition, black high-risk children who attended Head Start had lower crime rates than did black high-risk children who attended no preschool. In contrast, lower-risk children who attended preschool other than Head Start had no significant gains in high school graduation rates, college attendance, earnings, or lower crime rates relative to comparable low-risk children who attended no preschool.

The lack of significant benefits from non-Head Start preschool for low-risk kids that Garces, Thomas, and Currie (2000) found must be considered with caution because we have no data on the quality of the non-Head Start programs the children attended. If their findings for low-risk children reflect the relatively lower quality of the private preschools they attended, then low-risk children moving from non-high-quality private preschools to high-quality public prekindergarten may get some, all, or nearly all of the benefits associated with a high-quality program.

Studies of children born more recently, based on data sets of generally better quality, have been unambiguous in finding positive outcomes of prekindergarten attendance. Analyses of Georgia's preschool programs (Henry et al. 2003a and Henry et al. 2005) indicate that children from all economic backgrounds benefit from preschool. Specifically, they found that children in Georgia attending publicly funded prekindergarten, Head Start, and private preschools made significant gains from the beginning of preschool to the end of first grade on a variety of tests compared to national samples of children their age. Thus, children in Georgia who attended preschool *gained* relative to representative national samples of children, in which only about two-thirds of children attended some preschool. They also found that the gains across family income were greater the higher the quality of the preschool program. On 11 out of 16 measures, children attending Georgia's publicly funded prekindergarten program improved more than did the relatively poor children in the state's Head Start program or the relatively well-to-do children in private preschools, but the differences were not statistically significant. Henry et al. (2003a and 2005) also found that the quality of the public programs was higher on average than that of the private programs.

Evaluations of Oklahoma's universal prekindergarten program (Gormley and Gayer 2005; Gormley et al. 2004) also indicate that children from all economic backgrounds benefit from prekindergarten. Poorer children tended to gain more than richer children, but the differences in gains were not large. In addition, some of the largest gains appear to have been experienced by lower middle-income children—those who live in families with incomes between 1.3 and 1.85 times poverty-level income, which is greater than the income of families in which the bottom quarter of children reside. Also, it should be noted that the children who attended the state's universal prekindergarten were compared to children who had not attended the universal prekindergarten but who may have attended some other form of preschool such as private preschool or Head Start. Thus, the gains that were measured reflect the benefits of attending a relatively high-quality public prekindergarten program compared to the gains of attending, on average, lower quality preschool or no preschool at all.

Another interesting point about the Oklahoma universal prekindergarten program, which enrolls the majority of the state's four-year-olds and is only somewhat lower in quality than the Chicago CPC program, is that its estimated effects on the school readiness of high-risk children are similar in size to those of the Chicago CPC program, which enrolled only high-risk children. Thus, the results of the Oklahoma program may be similar enough to those of the Chicago CPC program to reasonably project that the effects of a Chicago-style universal prekindergarten program on middle- and upper-income children will be similar to its effects on low-income children, as in Oklahoma.[50]

Bridges et al. (2004) compared children in California who had attended preschool to those who had not attended any preschool. They found that the children who attended preschool had greater reading and math skills when they entered kindergarten than the children who had not attended preschool. They also found that the gains from preschool attendance were essentially the same for middle-income and low-risk children as they were for more disadvantaged children.

Studies in Canada and England also found that children who attended prekindergarten had better academic outcomes than children who did not attend preschool, regardless of their economic background (Lipps and Yipton-Avila 1999; Hersch 2004; Sammons et al. 2002 and 2003). Likewise, a study of the French prekindergarten program (Hirsch 2004) found that children gain from attending additional years of pre-K, and that these benefits are similar across income levels.

Barnett, Lamy, and Jung (2005), in an analysis of kindergarten children in five states, found that one year of state-funded, relatively high-quality prekindergarten significantly raised scores on vocabulary, print awareness, and math tests compared to children who did not attend the state-funded program. They found a somewhat stronger effect of prekindergarten on the print awareness of low-income children, but the improvements in math and vocabulary tests were virtually identical for children from high- and low-income families. Note, too, that many of the children in the comparison groups attended preschool programs other than the relatively high-quality, state-funded prekindergarten. Thus, this study also suggests that higher quality preschool programs provide benefits beyond those achieved by other preschool programs for children from all economic backgrounds (although in one area the greatest gains were for low-income children).

In a nationwide analysis, Magnuson et al. (2004 and 2005) found that children who attended preschool were better prepared and performed better in kindergarten than did students who did not attend preschool, regardless of economic background. However, they found that the greatest math and reading gains were achieved by the most disadvantaged children. On the other hand, the reduction in grade retention was roughly the same for high- and non-high-risk children. Magnuson et al. (2004) also provide estimates for the effects on reading and math skills of preschool participation relative to non-participation for the full sample and a sub-sample of children living in poverty.

Comparing the coefficients for math and reading scores of the full sample to the scores of the poor children for those children who attended private preschool or public prekindergarten suggests that average-risk kids may get anywhere from 60% to 95% of the benefits of preschool that are received by high-risk kids.

Several points are clear:

1. Children benefit from preschool education. This is generally true for children from poor, middle-, and upper-income families.
2. Higher quality preschool education programs provide greater benefits than lower quality preschool education programs.
3. Studies differ on the degree of impact that preschool education has on children from different economic backgrounds. Some studies find that the positive effects of preschool education on children from more- and less-advantaged backgrounds are nearly identical. Other studies suggest that children from low-income families gain more from preschool education than do children from middle- and high-income families. One study, the Oklahoma study (Gormley et al. 2004), suggests that for some skills lower-middle income children gain more than poorer or wealthier children.

Although it is clear that children benefit from high-quality prekindergarten, given the mixed results on the relative effects of preschool on children from different economic backgrounds, it is not certain to what extent the benefits of a high-quality, universal program modeled after the Chicago CPC program, that served high-risk children (from low-income families), would apply to medium-risk children (from middle-income families), and low-risk children (from high-income families) who would otherwise attend no preschool. Thus, we offer high-, low-, and intermediate- (or most likely) range estimates of these possible effects. In the main text, the intermediate range estimates were used, but a sensitivity analysis was performed to demonstrate what effect different estimates have on the final results.

For the high-end estimate we assume that the effects of prekindergarten are virtually identical for children of all economic backgrounds. Thus, we assume that all children in a universal, high-quality prekindergarten program who would otherwise have attended no preschool would get 100% of the prekindergarten effects measured in the Chicago CPC program. This is the assumption used by Dickens, Sawhill, and Tebbs (2006) when estimating the impact of a high-quality universal prekindergarten program on economic growth. In our high-end estimates of the costs and benefits of universal prekindergarten, moving from the baseline targeted-program-estimates to the universal-program-estimates, the costs and benefits are attenuated only to account for the disproportionate incidence of academic and social problems experienced by low-income, high-risk children (the baseline effect).

For our low-end estimate we assume that, while all children benefit from high-quality prekindergarten compared to attending no preschool, children from middle-income and wealthy families would experience much less improvement from prekindergarten than did the relatively disadvantaged children in the Chicago CPC program. Thus, for the low estimate we assume that middle-income children (who would otherwise have attended no preschool) would receive on average only 70% and upper-income children (who would otherwise have attended no preschool) would experience on average only 40% of the improvement estimated for the targeted prekindergarten program.

Our low-end estimate may appear to be higher than the assumption used by Karoly and Bigelow (2005) when estimating the impacts of a high-quality universal pre-K program in California. They assumed that medium-risk children (who would otherwise have attended no preschool) would receive on average only 50% and low-risk children (who would otherwise have attended no preschool) would experience on average only 25% of the benefits that high-quality pre-K confers on high-risk children. This is because we handle our calculations differently, applying the effect of the baseline distribution separately. Our low-end estimate may actually imply a smaller impact of pre-K on many outcomes for medium-risk and low-risk children than does Karoly and Bigelow's estimate once our initial baseline adjustment is taken into account.

Finally, for our intermediate estimate, we assume that all children benefit from high-quality prekindergarten, but children from middle-income and wealthy families would experience somewhat lower benefits from pre-K than did the relatively disadvantaged children attending the Chicago CPC program. Thus, for the intermediate estimate we assume that middle-income children (who would otherwise have attended no preschool) receive on average only 85% and upper income children (who would otherwise have attended no preschool) experience on average only 70% of the benefits estimated in the targeted prekindergarten program.

These attenuations are applied on top of adjustments for the baseline, or "room for improvement" effect, so the true attenuation for middle- and upper-income children is significantly higher. Specifically, in our estimating procedure for the costs and benefits of universal pre-K, we adjust these numbers to take into account that there is an inverse relationship between potential benefits experienced and family income. Thus, the estimating procedure calculates benefits of prekindergarten per low- and mid-risk children that are far less than 70% to 85% of those for high-risk children. For example, with the baseline adjustments, we assume that middle-income children receive on average only 49% and upper-income children experience only 40% of the reduction in child maltreatment rates experienced by relatively disadvantaged children.

Our intermediate estimate, which reflects an attenuation in the impact of prekindergarten on mid- and low-risk children, is consistent with the findings of Gormley et al. (2004) with respect to the relative benefits of the Oklahoma prekindergarten program for low-income children (those who qualified for free lunch) and financially advantaged children (those who paid full-price for lunch). Specifically, on tests of letter identification, spelling, and applied problems, the relatively financially advantaged children experienced improvements that were 78%, 83%, and 64%, respectively, as great as the improvements experienced by the relatively poor children.[51] We based our most likely intermediate estimates in part on the Oklahoma results because the Oklahoma universal prekindergarten program, which serves most of the four-year-olds in the state, is similar to, although somewhat lower in quality than, the Chicago CPC program. In addition, as noted earlier about the Oklahoma universal program, its estimated initial effects on school readiness of high-risk children are similar in size to those estimated for the initial effects of the Chicago CPC program on high-risk children. Thus, for both reasons it may be reasonable to assume that the effects of the Oklahoma program on middle and upper income children will be similar to those of a Chicago CPC-style universal program on middle- and upper-income children. However, it should be noted that the children who attended Oklahoma's universal prekindergarten were compared to children who had not attended the universal prekindergarten, but who may have attended some other form of preschool such as private preschool or Head Start. Thus, the gains that were measured for the Oklahoma participants reflect the benefits of attending a relatively high-quality prekindergarten program compared to the gains of attending, on average, a combination of lower quality preschool and no preschool at all. Since we are trying to measure the impact of a high-quality prekindergarten program on middle-income and high-income children who would otherwise attend no preschool, and given that middle- and high-income children who did not attend the Oklahoma program are more likely to have attended some other preschool, basing our estimate on the outcomes of the Oklahoma program is likely to result in overly conservative estimates of the benefits for mid- and low-risk children.

Our intermediate estimates are also reasonably consistent with the findings of Magnuson et al. (2004) who provide estimates of the effects of preschool participation relative to non-participation on average children and on children living in poverty. Comparing the coefficients for math and reading scores, their findings suggest that average children who attend preschool may get anywhere from 60% to 95% of the benefits of preschool that are received by high-risk children.

The average reduction in the benefits from prekindergarten for middle-income and upper-income children relative to poor children reflects at least two factors. One is that relatively well-to-do children may have lower baseline involvement in and use of a variety of services (such as child welfare or criminal justice services). The other factor is that pre-K may have a smaller impact on improving the academic and social skills of relatively well-to-do children compared to poor children in problem areas (such as special education and grade retention). Our estimating procedure takes into account both of these factors, using a *variable specific* (e.g., juvenile crime or grade repetition) estimate for the first factor based on data for the diverse levels of social and academic problems experienced by children from different family incomes, and an *average* estimate for the second factor, the relative impact of pre-K on children from different family incomes as described above. It is likely, however, that the impact of pre-K on non-high-risk children varies from problem area to problem, as does the baseline distribution. Thus, while our estimate of the *average* reduction in pre-K impacts for non-high-risk children may be accurate in the aggregate, it is likely that it will overstate the reduction in prekindergarten impacts in some areas and understate the reduction in impacts for non-high-risk children in others. Hence, we have somewhat more confidence in our estimates of the total benefits of the universal program than we do in the benefits associated with savings in any specific area, such as in special education, grade retention, criminal justice, or child welfare.

Attenuation of prekindergarten effects to account for current preschool enrollment

To calculate the benefits of targeted and universal prekindergarten we must estimate the extent to which the benefits of a high-quality pre-K program (like the Chicago CPC program) that compared outcomes for children who attended a high-quality prekindergarten program to outcomes for children who (for the most part) attended no preschool will apply to children who would otherwise attend some form of preschool. Roughly 85% of the children in the Chicago CPC program control group did not attend any preschool, while about 15% did attend preschool (mostly Head Start). Thus, to a large extent, but not completely, the Chicago CPC results compare students who attended high-quality prekindergarten to children in the control group who attended no preschool. In the United States, about half of three- and four-year-olds are already attending some form of preschool. Hence, if the United States were to adopt a publicly funded, universal, high-quality prekindergarten, it is probable that many of the children who would attend such a program would have otherwise attended some form of public or private preschool. The research reviewed above suggests that many currently existing preschool programs provide benefits to participants relative to children who do not attend preschool. Thus, the prospective positive effects of a high-quality, universal prekindergarten program should be attenuated to take into account that many of its prospective participants would attend some form of preschool and receive some of the benefits of prekindergarten in the absence of the universal program.[52]

A key question, therefore, is how much should we reduce the expected benefits of a prospective high-quality prekindergarten program for its participants who would in any case have attended some form of preschool?

The quality of preschool is clearly an important determinant of children's outcomes. Peisner-Feinberg et al. (2001) found that higher quality preschool programs had better results for children from all walks of life. Children attending higher quality child-care centers had higher test scores in language and math and higher ratings by teachers in cognitive and attention skills in kindergarten and second grade. These advantages did not fade through the second grade. Similarly, the National Institute of Child Health and Human Development (NICHD) found that children, regardless of family income, who had experienced higher quality care, had significantly higher math, memory, and vocabulary skills than children who had experienced lower quality care. They too found that these advantages persisted through time. "Children who experienced better child care quality in the first four-and-a-half years of life continued to manifest somewhat greater academic achievement across the primary grades (third grade) than other children" (NICHD 2005, 564). Henry et al. (2003b and 2005) also found that the gains across family income were greater the higher the quality of the preschool program. Thus, children who would otherwise attend low-quality preschools should benefit more from a high-quality public prekindergarten program than children who would otherwise attend a high-quality preschool program.

Barnett (2002 and 2005) compared the average outcomes for special education and grade repetition for high-quality model preschool programs to the average outcomes for relatively lower quality (but still good quality) Head Start and public prekindergarten programs. The comparison suggests that the relatively lower quality programs achieved about 25% of the reduction in special education and 55% of the reduction in grade repetition achieved by the higher quality programs. However, as Barnett noted, it may be misleading to compare these results as the higher quality programs were serving more disadvantaged children.

Dickens, Sawhill, and Tebbs (2006) assumed that children who would otherwise be enrolled in *private* preschool would receive no additional benefit from attending a high-quality publicly funded prekindergarten program, but children who would otherwise attend *public* preschool would get 50% of the additional benefits associated with high-quality public prekindergarten. Karoly and Bigelow (2005) assumed that low-risk (i.e., higher income) children who would otherwise be enrolled in *public* or *private* preschool would receive no additional benefit from attending a high-quality public prekindergarten program. They also assumed that high- and medium-risk children who would otherwise be enrolled in *private* preschool would receive no additional benefit from attending a high-quality, publicly funded prekindergarten while high- and medium-risk children who would otherwise attend *public* preschool would get 50% of the benefits associated with high-quality public prekindergarten. Thus, both sets of researchers implicitly assumed that private preschools provide greater educational benefits than public preschools. But are private preschools, in fact, of higher quality than public preschools?

The quality of preschool education programs is typically measured according to two standards: a structural standard and a process standard. The structural standard measures characteristics of preschool education programs such as teacher-child ratios, teacher pay, teacher qualifications, and class size. The process standard measures experiences in the preschool such as the nature of teacher-child interactions (were they warm, positive, supportive, stimulating, etc.), the relationships with parents, the activities in the classroom, the instructional materials, the health and safety procedures that are followed, and the quality of the instruction (art, music, science, math, problem solving, language development, reasoning, etc. are emphasized). Thus, high-quality prekindergarten education programs have low ratios of children to teachers (10 to 1 or better), small class sizes (20 or lower), and highly paid, well-qualified teachers and staff. Teachers are typically required to have a bachelor's degree with a specialization in early childhood education, and assistant teachers are usually required to have at least a child development associate or equivalent degree. Both teachers and assistants are given opportunities to continue their professional development. Parental involvement is encouraged and cultivated. Good programs provide a meal and offer health services. The activities in the classroom and the instructional materials are varied with emphasis placed on quality instruction in a wide range of fields. Finally, high-quality prekindergarten programs include monitoring programs and site visits to ensure that quality standards are being implemented.

Ripple et al. (1999), Smith et al. (2003), and Blau (2001) report that public prekindergartens are high-quality relative to other preschools in terms of a variety of criteria such as class size, child-staff ratios, and teachers' pay and education. While evaluations of public Head Start programs often rank them low in terms of teachers' pay and education, they rank high in terms of health and nutrition services, social services and parental involvement (Ripple et al. 1999). On average, Currie (2001) reports that Head Start programs are of higher quality than most other preschool programs.

Numerous studies of private preschool programs found their educational quality to be highly variable and *lower* on average than the quality available in the public programs. Blau (2001) and Helburn and Bergmann (2002) reported that the average private preschool does not rate highly in terms of staff/child ratios and teacher's education. In terms of learning environment and child-caregiver interactions, they found that few private programs are high-quality and quality is low for many others. The Cost, Quality, and Child Outcomes Study (1995) found that less than half the private programs analyzed provided positive child-caregiver interactions and only 24% offered developmentally appropriate care. Schulman and Barnett (2005) argue that middle-income children from families too rich to qualify for publicly funded programs but too poor to be able to afford expensive private programs are often forced to attend low-cost private programs of low quality. Phillips et al. (1994) found that most private child care centers for middle-income children had poorer quality ratings than did publicly funded centers that served low-income families.

Magnuson et al. (2004a), Magnuson et al. (2004b), and Magnuson et al. (2005) reported that, while children in any kind of preschool performed better than children who attended no preschool, children in *public* prekindergartens had larger gains than children in all other forms of preschool.

Henry et al. (2003a and 2005) found that the quality of the public prekindergarten programs was higher on average than that of the private preschools in Georgia. Barnett et al. (2004, 15) report that the quality of private preschool programs "is highly variable and tends to be lower on average than for public programs."

These findings do not support the notion that private preschools may be of higher quality and have greater impacts on children than public preschools. The bottom line is that there is no reason to believe that private preschools are better than public preschools as assumed by Karoly and Bigelow (2005) and Dickens, Sawhill, and Tebbs (2006). On the contrary, there are data that suggest that private preschools may be of poor quality and not as good as public preschools. Some researchers have concluded that the quality of private preschools on average is so poor that they offer little or even no benefit to participants. This reflects the assumption that Barnett et al. (2006) implicitly make when they calculate that the benefits for children in California who would shift from private preschool to a high-quality public prekindergarten would be the same as for those who would shift from no preschool to a high-quality public prekindergarten.

We take a conservative middle road. We assume that existing private and public preschool education programs are, on average, of similar quality.[53] We also assume, as suggested by the evidence presented above, that most existing preschool programs, whether private or public, although they may be providing significant benefits are not of high quality.

There is certainly evidence that existing preschool programs (private and public) provide some important benefits to participants compared to children who attend no preschool. Hence, children moving from low- or medium-quality preschool to high-quality prekindergarten should not gain as much as children moving from no preschool to high-quality prekindergarten. However, given that there is little quantitative evidence to indicate exactly how much smaller the impacts of currently existing preschool programs would be compared to a prospective high-quality program, we provide a range of estimates: high, low, and intermediate (or most likely) estimates. In our estimates of the costs and benefits of a high-quality universal program presented in this study, we used the intermediate estimate.[54]

For our high estimate, we assume that children attending the high-quality public prekindergarten who would otherwise have attended some other preschool would receive about 90% of the benefits received by participating children who would have otherwise attended no preschool. This implies that most of the existing preschool programs are of low quality and not generating many benefits.

At the other extreme, we assume that children who would otherwise have been enrolled in some form of preschool in the absence of the universal program reap only 30% of the benefits of comparable children attending the universal program who would have otherwise attended no preschool. This implies that existing preschool programs are fairly high quality and generating a substantial portion of the benefits participants would obtain in a prospective high-quality program.

Finally, for our intermediate estimate we assume that children who would have attended some other preschool in the absence of this high-quality universal prekindergarten program would experience 60% of the effect experienced by comparable children who would otherwise have attended no preschool. This implies that we expect the universal program to be of greater quality than existing preschool programs and to generate improvements that are about two-and-a-half times as large as those produced in the average currently existing preschool program.

This 60% impact is higher than the 50% assumption adopted by Karoly and Bigelow (2005) for high- and medium-risk children and by Dickens, Sawhill, and Tebbs (2006) for all children who would otherwise have attended public preschool. But, we believe that our intermediate estimate is probably conservative as the initial effects of high-quality public prekindergarten programs on the school readiness of non-poor and poor children are *substantially more than two-and-a-half times as large* as the initial effects of medium quality public preschool programs (Barnett et al. 2006). For example, the effect size for the Woodcock Johnson Letter Word Identification Test was 0.22 for children attending Head Start, according to the National Head Start Impact Study, while it was 0.63 for non-poor children (those paying full-price lunch) and 0.81 for low-income children (those receiving free lunch) attending the relatively high-quality Oklahoma universal prekindergarten program. Similarly, the effect size for the Woodcock Johnson Spelling Test was 0.16 for children attending Head Start, according to the National Head Start Impact Study, while it was 0.54 for non-poor children and 0.65 for low-income children attending the Oklahoma prekindergarten program. Note that the children in the Head Start study, just as the children in the Oklahoma study, were being compared to children many of whom attended preschool. Thus, low-income children shifting from an average-quality preschool program like Head Start to our proposed high-quality program may be expected to experience at least 73% to 75%[55] and not just 60% of the prekindergarten effect experienced by low-income children who would otherwise have attended no preschool. Non-poor children shifting from an average-quality program like Head Start to our proposed high-quality prekindergarten program may be expected to realize at least 65% to 70%[56] and not just 60% of the prekindergarten benefits experienced by non-poor children who would otherwise have attended no preschool.

Enrollment rates

The enrollment rates in the prospective targeted and universal prekindergarten programs were calculated by different methods. These methods, first for the targeted program and then for the universal program, are described below.

Percentage of three- and four-year-olds who will attend the targeted prekindergarten program

We assumed that the targeted pre-K program will enroll all three- and four-year-old children who live in families with incomes that are 125% or less of family poverty level (FPL) income. In the United States, children in families with 125% or less of FPL income represent roughly 25% of all children. The proportion of relatively poor children, however, varies considerably from state to state. For example, the percentage of children who reside in families with incomes that are 125% or less of FPL income varies from approximately 11% in New Hampshire to almost 38% in Mississippi.

Percentage of three- and four-year-olds who will attend preschool and enroll in the universal prekindergarten program

According to the Current Population Survey of October 2004 (U.S. Census Bureau 2004c), 37.2% of three-year-olds and 61.7% of four-year-olds were enrolled in some form of preschool program. Another 1.5% of three-year-olds and 6.7% of four-year-olds attended kindergarten. Thus, roughly 49.8% of all three- and four-year-olds were enrolled in preschool, the Head Start Program, nursery school, a day-care center, prekindergarten, or some other preschool program and 4.2% attended kindergarten.

Preschool participation rates varied by income level. Approximately 42% of the poorest quarter of three- and four-year-old children attended some form of preschool. Among middle-income families, a little less than half of the three- and four-year-olds were enrolled in preschool ,while among the top 25% of families about two-thirds of three- and four-year-olds attended some form of preschool (U.S Census Bureau 2004c and author's calculations).

Enrollment is almost evenly divided between public and private preschool programs. According to the Census Bureau (U.S. Census Bureau 2004c), among three- and four-year-old children who attend some form of preschool approximately, 52.4% of them attend public preschool programs while about 47.6% attend private preschool programs.

Only two states offer publicly funded, voluntary, universal prekindergarten services: Oklahoma and Georgia. Both states offer universal prekindergarten for four-year-olds only.

In Oklahoma in 2004-05, 92.4% of four-year-olds were enrolled in public preschool programs (state prekindergarten, Head Start, or IDEA Preschool Grants programs). In Georgia in 2004-05, 67.4% of four-year-olds were enrolled in public preschool programs (state prekindergarten, Head Start, or IDEA Preschool Grants programs) (Barnett et al. 2005b).

For both states, an unknown number of four-year-old children attended private preschool programs so that the total enrollment of four-year-old children in preschool programs is higher than the numbers above indicate. For the state of Georgia, however, we do have a good indicator of the number of four-year-olds in private preschool. Georgia administers the Georgia Kindergarten Assessment Program-Revised (GPAK-R) tests to almost all kindergarten students. In 2000-01, Georgia reported the results of the GPAK-R tests by preschool experience as reported by parents of kindergarten children. The test results suggest that between 19% and 23% of Georgia kindergarten children had attended private preschool. (By comparison, about one-third of kindergarten children in the United States as a whole attended private preschool.) In 2000-01 as in 2004-05, about 67% of Georgia four-year-olds attended public preschool programs. Thus, assuming that private preschool enrollment rates in Georgia, as is the case for public preschool enrollment rates in Georgia, have not changed significantly since 2000-01 and adding the private preschool enrollment numbers from the 2000-01 GPAK-R results to the public preschool enrollment numbers for 2004-05, we estimate that approximately 86% to 90% of four-year-olds attend private or public preschool in Georgia.[57] In Oklahoma, there are numerous private and church affiliated preschool programs serving children between the age of zero and five with total enrollments running into the thousands. However, we were not able to obtain data on the number of children by age who are enrolled in these programs. However, if just one-fifth to one-fourth of the non-public-preschool attending four-year-olds are enrolled in these private preschools, then somewhere between 94% and 95% of four-year-olds are enrolled in public or private preschool in Oklahoma.

Five European nations provide publicly funded, voluntary, universal prekindergarten services for both three- and four-year-olds: Belgium, France, Italy, Spain, and the United Kingdom. In 2001-02, the participation rate in preprimary education of four-year-olds was essentially 100% in all five nations (it was 99.9% in the United Kingdom) (European Commission 2005). Other than for the program in the United Kingdom, which has been providing free early education to four-year-olds only since 1998, these publicly funded programs have been in existence much longer than the Oklahoma and Georgia programs and thus may indicate the enrollment levels that will be reached in Oklahoma and Georgia over time.

Except for the relatively new program in the United Kingdom, the participation rate of three-year-olds in 2001-02 was the same as or only slightly lower than it was for four-year-olds: 100% in France, 99.4% in Belgium, 99.3% in Italy, 93.0% in Spain, and 53.4% in the United Kingdom. The entitlement to free early education in the United Kingdom was only extended to all three-year-olds in April 2004. According to the most recent data, the enrollment of three-year-olds in England in early education reached 96% by 2005 (Department for Education and Skills 2006). Using this more recent data for England and assuming that it applies to the entire United Kingdom, the unweighted average enrollment rate of three-year-olds in these five European nations is 97.5%, just 2.5 percentage points less than the enrollment rate of four-year-olds.

It is impossible to know with certainty what the future enrollment rates in the United States will be in a prospective, voluntary, publicly funded, high-quality prekindergarten program. In addition, we have a long history and tradition of some parents choosing to send their children to private schools instead of public schools: In the United States, approximately 90% of kindergarten through 12th grade children attend public school while 10% attend private school (U.S. Census Bureau 2005). Hence, we will provide three projections for total *public and private* preschool enrollment rates: high, low, and intermediate projections that assume participation rates at the low end, high end, and the most likely point of a plausible range, respectively. For each of these three projections, we will further break down the estimated total preschool enrollment between high-quality *public* prekindergarten programs and *private* preschools. For the most likely intermediate estimate, we will assume that private preschool will account for 10% of all preschool enrollment, while for the high- and low-end estimates, we will assume that private preschool enrollment will make up 5% and 15%, respectively, of preschool enrollment.

The estimates of the costs and benefits of a universal program presented in this book use our most likely intermediate estimate.

The high projection assumes a *public and private* preschool participation rate of almost 98.8%. This is based on the 100% participation of four-year-olds and 97.5% participation of three-year-olds that prevails on average in the five European nations with voluntary, publicly funded, universal prekindergarten programs. For the high-end projection, we assume that 95% of children attending preschool will attend the high-quality public prekindergarten programs while 5% will attend private programs. Thus, our high-end estimate is that about 94% of three- and four-year old children will attend the high-quality, public prekindergarten programs and almost 5% will attend private preschool.

For the low-end projection, we estimate a *private and public* preschool participation rate of about 80%. This assumes a participation rate of 86% for four-year-olds and of 75% for three-year-olds. The projected four-year-old participation rate is based on the low end of the 86% to 90% estimated range of four-year-old preschool enrollment in Georgia, which is the lowest rate of participation for such children in the states or countries we reviewed above that have voluntary, universal, publicly funded prekindergarten programs. The estimated prospective 75% participation rate of three-year-olds is based on our calculation of the ratio of three-year-old to four-year-old *private* preschool participation in the United States. We then multiplied this ratio (.87) by our assumed 86% rate of four-year-old preschool participation (i.e. 23.3/26.9 times 86%), to arrive at our estimated prospective 75% rate of three-year-old preschool participation.[58]

For the low end projection, we assume that 85% of children attending preschool will attend the high-quality public program while 15% will attend private programs. Thus, our low-end estimate is that 68% of three- and four-year old children will attend high-quality public prekindergarten programs and 12% will attend private preschool.

Finally, for our intermediate or most likely projection, we estimate about a 90% enrollment rate in *public and private* preschool. This assumes a participation rate of 93% for four-year-olds and of 86% for three-year-olds. The estimated participation rates of three- and four-year-olds is the average of our high and low end estimates for three and four-year-old preschool participation.

Reflecting the 90/10 division in the United States between public and private kindergarten through 12th grade enrollment, for the intermediate projection we assume that 81% of children will attend the high-quality public prekindergarten program while 9% will attend private programs.

The intermediate estimate may be conservative because the high-quality prekindergarten program proposed in this study should be more attractive to parents and children than either the Oklahoma or the Georgia program as neither of the latter meet al.l the high standards of excellence of the program proposed in this study. Thus, it may be reasonable to expect that the enrollment rate of four-year-olds in our high-quality publicly funded program should equal or surpass that achieved in 2004-05 in Oklahoma (92.4%) and Georgia (67%) and approach the levels reached in Europe (100%). Instead, we are assuming that it will be 84% in the proposed program, well below the European level and between the Oklahoma and Georgia levels. We then expect, consistent with both the U.S. and the European experience, that the enrollment rate of three-year-olds in the public universal program (77%) will be close to, but somewhat lower than, the enrollment rate of four-year-olds.

The enrollment of children in the universal prekindergarten education program is further adjusted to take into account the likely differential enrollment rates of children from different family income backgrounds. In general, upper-income families are more likely to enroll their children in private preschool programs and less likely to enroll them in public prekindergarten programs than are middle-income or lower-income families. Thus, we adjust the participation rates to reflect the current weighting of enrollment rates by income distribution in public K-12 schooling. Since current public K-12 enrollment includes 99% of lower-income children, 90% of middle-income children, and 82% of upper-income children, the outcome of our weighting scheme leads to an over-representation of lower-income children and an under-representation of upper-income children in the universal program. Specifically, about 28% and 22% of the universal pre-K participants are assumed to come from low-income and high-income families respectively, while both these groups account for only 25% each of the population.

Accrual of costs and benefits through time

The costs and benefits detailed in this report are estimated as yearly flows over time. This is a relatively complicated endeavor because different benefits and costs accrue at different times in program participants' lives. For each year, the calculations include benefits and costs related to the current year's program participants, and all previous participants, all in the current year's dollars, tracking a changing population. Below is a highly simplified example.

Consider a one year program for five-year-olds, costing the government $100 in 2006. The parents of these children agree to pay $200 when the children are six years old. The cost of the program increases due to inflation: in 2007 it costs $105, $110 in 2008, and $115 in 2009. The inflation seen by the parents is the same, raising their payments to $210 in 2007, $220 in 2008 and $230 in 2009. The population affected also increases: in 2006 there are five five-year-olds, in 2007 there are six, in 2008 there are seven, and in 2009 there are eight. These are the only costs and benefits accrued to the government.

What is the affect of this program on government finances in each year? In each year, the cost is equal to the number of five-year-olds multiplied by the per-child cost (**Table B1**). Similarly, in each year the benefits of the program are equal to the per-child payment multiplied by the number of six-year-olds, or the number of five-year-olds from one year earlier (**Table B2**). Thus, the program generates a net expenditure of $500 in 2006, but in 2007 generates net revenue of $1000-$630= $370. The net revenue increases in 2008 to $1320-$770= $550, and in 2009 increases to $1610-$920= $690.

This basic method is used to calculate the yearly net benefit flows provided by prekindergarten programs. The costs calculated above are accrued over differing periods of a participant's life (**Table B3**). The program costs are already expressed as per year values. The other costs/benefits are essentially estimates of the sum of the per-year cost/benefit over the period, expressed in 2006 dollars. For example, we have calculated an average per-child savings for special education. Different children will require special education at different points in their educational careers, but over the course of their

TABLE B1 Program costs

Year	Per-child cost		five-year-olds		Total cost
2006	$100	X	5	=	$500
2007	$105	X	6	=	$630
2008	$110	X	7	=	$770
2009	$115	X	8	=	$920

Source: Author's analysis.

TABLE B2 Program benefits

Year	Per-child payment		six-year-olds		Total benefit
2006	-	X	-	=	-
2007	$200	X	5	=	$1,000
2008	$220	X	6	=	$1,320
2009	$230	X	7	=	$1,610

Source: Author's analysis.

careers the participants will, on average, create the estimated savings from reduced special education use.

They will create these savings sometime between the ages of five and 17. It is assumed that the special education savings due to a given *child* can occur at any point during this period, but that the total special education savings due to a given *cohort* is spread roughly evenly over these years. So, the initial special education savings estimate is divided by the 13 years in the benefit accrual period, yielding the average per-year per-child savings. The total savings in a given year is calculated by multiplying this per-year per-child savings by the total number of participants falling within the given age range in the given year, and inflating this savings to current-year dollars. This savings will change each year as the age range encompasses a different cohort, increasing rapidly at first to account for the first cohorts moving progressively further into the age range in question, then more slowly once the range is entirely occupied but the cohorts tracking through continue to grow with population growth. All costs and benefits are assumed to maintain real value, growing each year with projections of the relevant inflation indexes. This inflation would be unnecessary if we did not assume different inflation for different cost/benefit components.

The case of adult crime savings is somewhat more complicated than the rest, as criminal activity is *not* distributed evenly across a criminal career. For the purposes of this model, adult crime costs at age 18 are multiplied by 0.8 to get the effect of juvenile crime savings on adult crime savings (Greenwood et al. 1998 and Karoly et al. 1998). It is further assumed that peak adult criminal activity occurs at age 18, and that criminal activity decreases by 10% each year until it ceases at age 45 (Greenwood et al. 1998 and Karoly et al. 1998). In order to accomplish this, a multiplier stream was applied to the average yearly per-person savings calculated above: a factor was created for each age within the range, using a goal-seek algorithm, such that the multiplier stream peaks in the first year of the age range, diminishes by 10% in each successive year,

TABLE B3 Participants ages over which costs and benefits accrue

	Age
Program costs	3-4
Increased high school	17
Increased higher ed	18-22
Decreased special ed	5-17
Decreased grade retention	17
Child welfare savings	3-17
Juvenile justice savings	10-17
Adult justice savings	18-44
Increased earnings of guardians	3-4
Increased earnings of participants	18-65
Increased taxes	18-65

Source: Reynolds et al. (2002) and author's analysis.

and sums to the number of years in the age range. The average value of this multiplier is one, so when it is applied to the per-year per-person savings calculated by dividing the per-person savings by the number of years in the age range, the sum of the products of the multiplier and the savings will equal the total estimated per-person savings, but more of the savings will be accrued up front. The savings from reduced adult crime in a given year was thus calculated by summing the products for each age in the age range of the number of program participants of that age in the given year, the per-person per-year savings, and the multiplier for that age.

In brief, the total costs and benefits of the preschool programs were determined by multiplying the number of participants of a particular age by the average value of the cost or benefit for each year the cost or benefit was produced by participants of that age as indicated in Table 9. Thus, for example, the costs of the prekindergarten program were assumed to prevail only when each participant was three- or four-years-old. The costs of increased high school education attainment were assumed to occur at age 17. The costs of higher education were assumed to start at age 18 and stop at age 22. The reductions in the cost of providing public education per participant, due to less special education, were assumed to kick in when that participant entered the public school system at age five and were assumed to cease when that participant turned 18 and left the school system. The savings from less grade retention were assumed to occur when participants were 17. The savings from less child abuse and neglect were assumed to start at age three and end at age 17. Savings from less juvenile crime were assumed to start at age 10 and end at age 17. Savings from less adult crime are assumed to start at age 18 and end at age 44. The benefits of higher earnings and taxes from the increased workforce participation of the guardians of pre-K participants were assumed to occur during the two years the participants were in prekindergarten. The benefits of higher earnings and taxes on the part of pre-K participants were assumed to start at age 18 and cease at age 65. Of course, all cost and benefits end in the year 2050, regardless of the age of prekindergarten participants in that year, as 2050 is the last year of our extrapolation.

Endnotes

1. In 2004, a family consisting of a single parent with two children was officially considered poor if the family income was below $15,219; for two parents with two children the poverty level income threshold was $19,157.
2. National Center for Children in Poverty, www.nccp.org/pub_cpt05b.html.
3. The fifth country that ranked lower than the United States on all three measures was Italy.
4. The 14 economically advanced countries assessed by the OECD are Australia, Belgium, Canada, Denmark, Finland, Germany, Ireland, Netherlands, New Zealand, Norway, Sweden, Switzerland, the United Kingdom, and the United States. The other six nations are Chile, the Czech Republic, Hungary, Poland, Portugal, and Slovenia.
5. The summary is available at www.hrsdc.gc.ca/en/hip/lld/nls/Surveys/ialsfrh.shtml.
6. See The Disaster Center at www.disastercenter.com.
7. For a review of this literature, see Ashenfelter and Rouse (1999).
8. See Appendix B on methodology for a description of the elements of high-quality preschool education programs.
9. For more details on the benefits of ECD programs, see chapter 2.
10. All but the Chicago Child-Parent Center program had random assignment of potentially eligible children into the intervention program or the control group. The analysis of the Chicago CPC program began after the children had been accepted into the program. The outcomes for the treatment group were then compared to the outcomes for a control group of children selected from Chicago neighborhoods that met the eligibility requirements but did not have a CPC prekindergarten program. Thus, the Chicago Child-Parent Center program did not use randomized assignment into intervention and the control group, but the control group did closely match the intervention group on age, eligibility for intervention, and family socioeconomic status. However, only 60% of the Chicago CPC children subsequently attended full day kindergarten whereas *all* the control group children did, possibly introducing a conservative bias in the outcome effects of the CPC program.
11. Of course, given financial constraints it may not be possible to invest in all projects with benefit-cost ratios greater than 1 to 1.
12. It was not always possible to monetize the benefits that were identified (such as the monetary benefit of reduced illegal drug usage), and not all the likely benefits were identified and monetized (such as the increased employment and earnings of parents who had children enrolled in prekindergarten programs).
13. Masse and Barnett (2002) did not calculate government savings for the Abecedarian program. They did indicate budgetary impacts for government in the form of lower public education spending, lower welfare outlays, and increased outlays for public higher education. But Masse and Barnett did not estimate the tax revenues that would derive from the additional earnings that they calculated would be generated by participants and their families. Nor did

they calculate criminal justice system savings because their data on the Abecedarian program showed reductions in crime that were not statistically significant. If we ignore criminal justice system savings and apply a 33.3% marginal tax rate (e.g., 8% federal, 15.3% payroll, and 10% state and local taxes) to the additional earnings of participants and their families, then the benefit-cost ratio for government from the Abecedarian program would be 1.1 to 1.

14. See Barnett et al. (2005b) for a more detailed description of the features of a high-quality prekindergarten program.
15. As noted in the text, numerous other benefits were identified, but the differences between program and non-program groups were not always statistically significant. For example, rates of tobacco and marijuana/hashish usage were much lower among program participants than non-participants at age 40 (42% versus 55% for tobacco and 45% versus 54% for marijuana/hashish). By age 27, 7% of the preschoolers had been arrested five or more times as compared to 29% of those who had not participated in preschool. By age 40, 28% of program participants had been sentenced to prison compared to 52% of non-participants
16. Although the results were not statistically significant, on average, these young mothers had more education (11.9 years versus 10.3 years) than did the control group young mothers. Moreover, only 23% of these young mothers had an additional birth compared to 40% of the young mothers in the control group.
17. This and the above three paragraphs are drawn from http://www.waisman.wisc.edu/cls/History.htm; http://www.waisman.wisc.edu/cls/eligibil.htm; http://www.waisman.wisc.edu/cls/component.htm; and Reynolds 2000.
18. http://www.ecechicago.org/about/glance.html, retrieved 6/1/06.
19. http://www.waisman.wisc.edu/cls/component.htm, retrieved 5/22/06.
20. Given disadvantaged children's deprivation of these kinds of activities relative to what occurs for children in more advantaged families, it is interesting to note this deliberate effort by schools to develop CPC youngsters' social and cultural capital. Doris Entwistle and Karl Alexander have written about the importance of providing social and cultural capital to disadvantaged children. See, for example, Doris R. Entwisle, Karl L. Alexander, and Linda Steffel Olson, 2000, "Summer Learning and Home Environment," in Richard D. Kahlenberg, ed., *A Notion at Risk: Preserving Public Education as an Engine for Social Mobility*, New York: Century Foundation Press, pp. 9-30 (see esp., pp. 17-18 and 27-8); Doris R. Entwisle, Karl L. Alexander, and Linda Stefel Olson, 1997, *Children, Schools, and Inequality*, Boulder, Colo.: Westview Press; Tiffani Chin and Meredith Phillips, 2004, "Social reproduction and child-rearing practices: social class, children's agency, and the summer activity gap," *Sociology of Education*, Vol. 77 (July), pp. 185-210; James S. Coleman, 1988, "Social capital in the creation of human capital," *American Journal of Sociology*, Vol. 94, pp. 95-120.
21. Unless otherwise noted, all material in this section is drawn from Graue et al. 2004.
22. Ibid.
23. See also http://www.waisman.wisc.edu/cls/parent.htm.
24. See, for example, Wendy T. Miedel and Arthur J. Reynolds, "Parent Involvement in Early Intervention for Disadvantaged Children: Does It Matter?" paper presented at Head Start's Fourth Annual Research Conference, July 10, 1998, *Journal of School Psychology*, Vol. 37, No 4, p. 379-402, abstract retrieved from http://www.waisman.wisc.edu/cls/Article1.htm, 5/23/06; Miedel and Reynolds, "Parent Involvement in Elementary School and High-School

Success: Is There a Connection?", paper presented at SRCD Research Conference, April, 1999, abstract retrieved from http://www.waisman.wisc.edu/cls/article4.htm; and Arthur Reynolds and Melissa Clements, "Parent Involvement and Children's School Success," in Patrikakou et al., *School-Family Partnerships: Promoting the Social, Emotional, and Academic Growth of Children*, New York: Teachers College Press, 2005, citation and summary retrieved from www.centerforparentleadership.org/Arthur%20Reynolds.study1.doc.

25. For the sake of efficiency, the program could run two sessions per day (a morning and an afternoon session). In addition, to meet the needs of parents, it could provide wraparound child care services paid for by funds not included in this analysis such as from existing public child care subsidies or from families themselves.
26. The program is voluntary to respect the decisions of parents who would choose not to enroll their children in an education program, to allow for home-schooling or attendance at a religious or other private preschool, and to account for the medical or other special needs of children.
27. These benefits of a targeted program are similar in magnitude to those estimated in Lynch (2004) for a targeted program modeled on the Perry Preschool program.
28. This results in states paying 95% and the federal government picking up 5% of the net program costs.
29. Thus, it may be a wise budgetary strategy for the federal government to provide incentives to states to encourage them to provide prekindergarten programs.
30. In the unlikely case where the federal government refused to pay for any of the costs of the prekindergarten program *and* did not allow states to spend any federal Head Start or special education monies on the program, it would still be a good investment from the limited perspective of state budget savings. States as a whole would experience net budget savings within 14 years, and by 2050 every state tax dollar spent on the program would be offset by $1.56 in budgetary savings for state governments in that year. Similarly, if state governments refused to pay for any of the costs of the prekindergarten program *and* did not allow the federal government to apply state savings in Head Start, special education, and other state prekindergarten expenditures to the program, the federally financed pre-K program would be a good investment from the narrow perspective of federal budgetary savings. In these circumstances, the federal government would experience net budget savings within 33 years and by 2050, every federal tax dollar spent on the program would be offset by $1.36 in budgetary savings for the federal government.
31. The estimates of budgetary, economic and crime effects of investment in preschool education are not as precise at the individual state level as they are at the nationwide level because, for some variables, state specific data were not available by state or for every state. In such circumstances, national averages were used to approximate state data.
32. Alabama's relatively low numbers are primarily due to low current state spending on these programs and low tax burden, not low benefits from the program.
33. In the extreme circumstance that the federal government refuses to pay for any of the costs of the prekindergarten program and cuts federal funding in Head Start and special education expenditures rather than letting states apply savings to the costs of the program, the program would still be a worthwhile investment from the narrow perspective of state budgetary savings for 49 of 50 states. These states would experience net budget savings in as few as

eight years in Connecticut and Delaware, and in no more than 34 years in Indiana. The only exception is Alabama, which relies heavily on federal Head Start funds to finance its limited preschool programs. By 2050, every Alabama tax dollar expended on the program would return 90 cents in budget savings. Of course, Alabama taxpayers and federal taxpayers collectively would still experience net budget savings if Alabama paid the entire costs of the prekindergarten program. For the other 49 states, by 2050 every state taxpayer dollar invested in the program would generate at least $1.07 in budgetary savings (for Indiana) and as much as $2.79 in budget savings in Connecticut.

34. Given our calculations in endnote 13, non-government benefits account for 81.3% of the total benefits of the Abecedarian program.
35. See the methodology in the appendix for an explanation of how this monetization is accomplished.
36. The program is voluntary to respect the decisions of parents who would choose not to enroll their children in an education program, to allow for home-schooling or attendance at a religious or other private preschool, and to account for the medical or other special needs of children.
37. In such circumstance, states would pay 95% and the federal government would pay 5% of the net costs of the program.
38. In the unlikely scenario that the federal government refused to pay for any of the costs of the universal prekindergarten program and did not allow states to apply federal savings in Head Start and special education to offset some of the costs of the program, by 2050 the universal program would return $1.09 for every state tax dollar spent in that year. While state budgets as a whole would be slightly more than breaking even, the federal government would be amassing $87 billion in surplus revenue in 2050 from the effects of the universal preschool program.

    In the equally unlikely scenario that state governments refused to pay for any of the costs of the pre-K program and refused to allow the federal government to apply state savings in Head Start, special education, and other state prekindergarten expenditures to offset some of the costs of the program, in 2050 the program would return 88 cents for every federal tax dollar invested in it. On top of the return to the federal government, states would be running $107 billion in surpluses.
39. The estimates of budgetary, economic, and crime effects of investment in pre-K are not as precise at the individual state level as they are at the nationwide level because, for some variables, state specific data were not available by state or for every state. In such circumstances, national averages were used to approximate state data.
40. Of course, if the federal government picks up the costs for the preschool program, then state budgets benefit enormously whether or not states maintain their efforts in preschool, Head Start, and special education. For example, if the federal government pays for the program and states simply maintain their efforts, then collectively, state governments experience $94 billion in budget surpluses by 2050.

    Also, in the unlikely circumstance that the federal government refused to pay for any of the costs of the preschool program and refused to allow states to apply federal savings in Head Start and special education expenditures to offset some of the costs of the program, the program would still produce budget surpluses in 30 states and a federal surplus of $87 billion by 2050. By 2050, state budgets as a whole would more than break even ($1.09 in offsetting budget savings for each dollar spent), but every Alabama tax dollar expended on the program would return only 68 cents in budget savings while every state tax dollar invested in the program would generate $1.60 in budgetary savings for the state of New York.

41. In other sensitivity analyses, we also varied the prospective enrollment rate in the universal program from a high of 94% to a low of 68% compared to the 81% assumed in the estimates presented in this study. Higher enrollment rates, by scaling both costs and benefits, produced somewhat larger estimates of budget surpluses, compensation increases, and crime savings compared to the 81% enrollment rate estimate. However, they also generated somewhat lower estimates of the ratio of budget benefits to budget costs and thus slightly lower rates of return on each tax dollar invested in the program in 2050. Lower enrollment rates produced somewhat smaller estimates of budget surpluses, compensation increases, and crime savings. Yet, they also generated somewhat higher estimates of the ratio of budget benefits to budget costs.
42. Our most likely estimate of the effect of universal pre-K assumes 40% attenuation to account for the effects of current preschool enrollment rates and impacts on middle- and upper-income children that are 85% and 70% of those for the Chicago CPC participants. It suggests that universal pre-K investment would generate a net budgetary surplus of $96 billion in 2050 and that every dollar spent in 2050 would return $2.00 in budget savings in that year. The increase in compensation is estimated to amount to $432 billion per year and the savings to individuals from less crime equal $156 billion in 2050.
43. Note that we assume that the prekindergarten program (whether targeted or universal) is launched simultaneously in all states in 2007. In this way, the net transference of program costs and benefits between states as prekindergarten participants and their families move across state borders is likely to be very small and can be ignored. If states were not to simultaneously launch pre-K programs, then states without public pre-K programs but with in-migration would likely experience some of the benefits of prekindergarten paid for by other states. Similarly, states with public pre-K programs and out-migration would likely lose some of the benefits of pre-K that they had paid for.
44. From the program costs, we subtracted the imputed opportunity costs for parent participation that were based on an assumed 10 hours of parent participation per month at the then-prevailing minimum wage of $3.35 per hour. This parental time cost was subtracted because it is not a cost to government.
45. This should not be interpreted as a method of estimating the marginal return to a high school diploma. We are essentially using the marginal returns to high school-or-greater educational attainment as an instrument for all of the observable and unobservable characteristics affected by prekindergarten investment that influence earnings later in life.
46. See www.bls.gov/cew/home.htm.
47. The processes of determining the increases in the earnings and compensation of pre-K participants and their guardians were described in the paragraphs above that explain the tax revenue increases accruing to government from pre-K investment. These descriptions will not be repeated here.
48. Of course, while rates of problems may be higher for lower-income children, total incidence of problems is generally greater for middle- and upper-income children because there are more of them.

49. One has to be somewhat careful in interpreting these data because the greater school readiness of more advantaged children may, in part, reflect that they are more likely to have attended prekindergarten than are less advantaged children. In other words, the degree of school readiness may be more similar than the data above suggest for samples of children from different economic backgrounds who have the same pre-K participation rates.

50. Although as Barnett et al. (2006) note, the effects of the Chicago CPC prekindergarten program may be underestimated because the comparison group in the Chicago study had access to high-quality full-day kindergarten.

51. For children receiving the full-price lunch, the letter-word identification scores increased by 0.63 of the standard deviation for the control group; spelling scores increased 0.54 of the standard deviation for the control group; and the applied problems scores increased by 0.29 of the standard deviation of the control group. By comparison, for children receiving free lunch, the letter-word identification scores increased by 0.81 of the standard deviation for the control group; spelling scores increased 0.65 of the standard deviation for the control group; and the applied problems scores increased by 0.45 of the standard deviation of the control group.

52. A similar attenuation was made for the targeted program to take into account that many of its prospective participants would attend some form of preschool and receive some of the benefits of prekindergarten in the absence of the targeted program. The attenuation methodology is the same for the targeted program as it is for the universal program and is described once in this section of the paper.

53. Recent evidence from the U.S. Department of Education, National Center for Education Statistics (2006) supports the notion that private schools on average are no more effective than public schools. Adjusted for the characteristics of children (such as race and gender), children in a survey of some 6,000 public schools scored higher in grade four mathematics, equally well in grade four reading and grade eight mathematics, and less well on grade eight reading than did children in a survey of over 500 private schools.

54. In our cost and benefit estimating procedure, when attenuating the potential benefits to account for prior preschool attendance we do not factor out the fact that 15% of the Chicago CPC program control group attended preschool. Thus, our attenuation for prior preschool attendance may be too great.

55. The calculation based on effect sizes is as follows: (.81-.22)/.81=.73 or 73% and (.65-.16)/.65 = .75 or 75%.

56. The calculation based on effect sizes is as follows: (.63-.22)/.63 =.65 or 65% and (.54-.16)/.54 =.7 or 70%.

57. Children in private preschool programs in Georgia may be attending full-day, half-day, or only part-day and part-week. There are no data on the hours of private preschool enrollment in Georgia.

58. To estimate the participation rate of three-year-olds, we were tempted to use the 0.6 ratio of three-year-old preschool participation rate to four-year-old preschool participation rate in the United States multiplied by our assumed 86% rate of four-year-old preschool participation. But this struck us as an implausibly low estimate given that 11 of the 38 states that make public prekindergarten available to four-year-olds do not offer public prekindergarten services to three-year-olds (Barnett et al. 2005b, 7, Table 1). In addition, nearly every state makes a

smaller financial commitment to preschool for three-year-olds than they do to preschool programs for four-year-olds. By contrast, in our proposed prekindergarten program there will be equal access to public prekindergarten for three and four-year-olds and this should have an equalizing effect on the rates of three- and four-year-old preschool participation. Given that the U.S. ratio of three-year-old to four-year-old preschool participation rate is partly driven by public policy choices and not just parental choices, we felt that it would be more accurate to predict the prospective enrollment rate of three-year-olds based on our calculation of the ratio of three-year-old to four-year-old *private* preschool participation rate in the United States.

Bibliography

Anderson, Patricia M., and Philip B. Levine. 2000. "Child Care and Mothers' Employment Decisions," in Rebecca M. Blank and David Card, eds., *Finding Jobs: Work and Welfare Reform*. New York, N.Y.: Russell Sage Foundation.

Aos, Steven, Roxanne Lieb, Jim Mayfield, Marna Miller, and Annie Pennucci. 2004. *Benefits and Costs of Prevention and Early Intervention Programs for Youth*. Olympia, Wash.: Washington State Institute for Public Policy. http://www.wsipp.wa.gov/rptfiles/04-07-3901.pdf http://www.wsipp.wa.gov/rptfiles/04-07-3901a.pdf.

Ashenfelter, Orley, Colm Harmon, and Hessel Oosterbeek. 1999. "A review of estimates of the schooling/earnings relationship, with tests for publications bias." *Labour Economics*. Vol. 6, No. 4, pp. 453-70. November.

Ashenfelter, Orley, and Cecilia Rouse. 1999. *Schooling, Intelligence, and Income in America: Cracks in the Bell Curve*. National Bureau of Economic Research Working Paper No. 6902. Cambridge, Mass.: NBER.

Aughinbaugh, Alison. 2001. Does Head Start yield long-term benefits? *Journal of Human Resources*. Vol. 36, No. 4, pp. 641-65.

Barclay, G., and Tavares, C. 2003. *International Comparisons of Criminal Justice Statistics 2001*. London: Home Office, Research Development Statistics. http://www.homeoffice.gov.uk/rds/pdfs2/hosb1203.pdf.

Barnett, W. Steven. 1993. Benefit-cost analysis of preschool education: Findings from a 25-year follow-up. *American Journal of Orthopsychiatry*. Vol. 63, No. 4, pp. 500-8.

Barnett, W. Steven. 1995. Long-term effects of early childhood programs on cognitive and school outcomes. *The Future of Children*. Vol. 5, No. 3, pp. 25-50.

Barnett, W. Steven. 2002. *The Battle Over Head Start: What the Research Shows*. New Brunswick, N.J.: National Institute for Early Education Research.

Barnett, W. Steven. 2004. "Does Head Start Have Lasting Cognitive Effects?: The Myth of Fadeout." In E. Zigler and S. Styfco, eds., *The Head Start Debates*. Baltimore, Md: Paul H. Brookes Publishing Company.

Barnett, W. Steven. 2005. "Maximizing Returns from Prekindergarten Education." In *Federal Reserve Bank of Cleveland Research Conference: Education and Economic Development*. Cleveland, Ohio: Federal Reserve Bank of Cleveland. pp. 5-18.

Barnett, W. Steven, Debra J. Ackerman, and Kenneth B. Robin. 2006. *California's Preschool for All Act (Proposition 82): A Policy Analysis*. New Brunswick, N.J.: National Institute for Early Education Research. May 18.

Barnett, W. Steven, and Donald Yarosz. 2004. Who goes to preschool and why does it matter? *Preschool Policy Matters*. New Brunswick, N.J.: National Institute for Early Education Research. Issue 8, August.

Barnett, W. Steven, Kirsty Brown, and Rima Shore. 2004. The universal vs. targeted debate: Should the United States have preschool for all? *Preschool Policy Matters*. New Brunswick, N.J.: National Institute for Early Education Research. Issue 6. April.

Barnett, W. Steven, and Jason T. Hustedt. 2005. Head Start's lasting benefits. *Infants & Young Children*. Vol. 18, No. 1. pp. 16-24.

Barnett, W. Steven, Jason T. Hustedt, Kenneth B. Robin, and Karen L. Schulman. 2004. *The State of Preschool: 2004 State Preschool Yearbook*. New Brunswick, N.J.: National Institute for Early Education Research.

Barnett, W. Steven, Jason T. Hustedt, Kenneth B. Robin, and Karen L. Schulman. 2005. *The State of Preschool: 2005 State Preschool Yearbook*. New Brunswick, N.J.: National Institute for Early Education Research.

Barnett, W. Steven, Cynthia Lamy, and Kwanghee Jung. 2005a. *The Effects of State Prekindergarten Prgrams on Young Children's School Readiness in Five States*. New Brunswick, N.J.: National Institute for Early Education Research. August.

Bartik, Timothy J. 2001. *Jobs for the Poor: Can Labor Policies Help?* New York, N.Y.: Russell Sage Foundation.

Bartik, Timothy J. 2006. *Taking Preschool Education Seriously as an Economic Development Program: Effects on Jobs and Earnings of State Residents Compared to Traditional Economic Development Programs*. Kalamazoo, Mich.: W.E. Upjohn Institute for Employment Research.

Bees, Roseana, Cynthia Andrews, Amy Jantz, Victoria Russell, and Rob Green. 2003. *The Cost of Protecting Vulnerable Children III: What Factors Affect States' Fiscal Decisions?* Occasional Paper No. 61. Washington D.C.: The Urban Institute.

Belfield, Clive R. 2004a. *Early Childhood Education: How Important Are the Cost-Savings to the School System?* Center for Early Care and Education, February.
http://www.winningbeginningny.org/databank/documents/belfield_report_000.pdf.

Belfield, Clive R. 2004b. *Investing in Early Childhood Education in Ohio: An Economic Appraisal.* Report prepared for Renewing Our Schools, Securing Our Future: A National Task Force on Public Education. Washington, D.C.: Center for American Progress. August. http://www.americanprogress.org/issues/2004/08/b172214.html.

Blanchflower, David, and Andrew Oswald. 2000. *Wellbeing Over Time in Britain and the U.S.A.* Working Paper. Cambridge, Mass.: National Bureau of Economic Research.

Blau, David M. 2001. *The Child Care Problem: An Economic Analysis.* New York, N.Y.: Russell Sage Foundation.

Blau, David M., and Allison Hagy. 1998. The demand for quality in child care. *Journal of Political Economy.* Vol. 106, No. 1, pp. 104-46.

Bridges, Margaret, Bruce Feller, Russell Rumberger, and Loan Tran. 2004. *Preschool for California's Children: Promising Benefits, Unequal Access.* PACE Policy Brief. Berkeley, Calif.: Policy Analysis for California Education.

Broberg, A.G., H. Wessel, M.E. Lamb, and C. P. Hwang. 1997. Effects of day care on the development of cognitive abilities in 8-year olds: A longitudinal study. *Developmental Psychology.* Vol. 33, pp. 62-9.

Burtless, Gary. 1999. "Risk and Returns of Stock Market Investments Held in Individual Retirement Accounts." Testimony before the House Budget Committee, Task Force on Social Security Reform. May 11.

Campbell, Frances A. 1995. Cognitive and school outcomes for high-risk African American students at middle adolescence: Positive effects of early intervention. *American Education Research Journal.* Vol. 32, No. 4, pp. 743-72.

Campbell, Frances A., and Craig T. Ramey. 1994. Effects of early intervention on intellectual and academic achievement: A follow-up study of children from low-income families. *Child Development.* Vol. 65, No. 2, pp. 684-9.

Campbell, Frances, Craig Ramey, Elizabeth Pungello, Joseph Sparling, and Shari Miller-Johnson. 2002. Early childhood education: Young adult outcomes from the abecedarian project. *Applied Development Science.*Vol. 6, No. 1, 42-57.

Carneiro, Pedro, Flavio Cunha, and James Heckman. 2003.*Interpreting the Evidence of Family Influence on Child Development.* Paper presented at The Economics of Early Childhood Development: Lessons for Economic Policy conference. Co-hosted by The Federal Reserve Bank of Minneapolis and The McKnight Foundation in cooperation with the University of Minnesota. October 17.

Center for the Study of Education Policy. 2004. *State and Local Appropriations for Higher Education, FY 2004.* Normal, Ill.: Grapevine, Illinois State University. Table 9.

Chicago Longitudinal Study. 1999. A *Study of Children in the Chicago Public Schools: User's Guide (Version 6).* Madison, Wisc.: University of Wisconsin.

Cicirelli,Victor G. 1969. *The Impact of Head Start: An Evaluation of the Effects of Head Start on Children's Cognitive and Affective Development.* Athens, Ohio and New York: Ohio University and Westinghouse Learning Corporation.

Committee for Economic Development. 2002. *Preschool for All: Investing in a Productive and Just Society*. New York, N.Y.: CED.

Committee for Economic Development. 2003. Paying for universal Pre-K. *CED in Brief.* http://www.ced.org/newsroom/inbrief/brief_preschool_feb03.pdf.

Committee for Economic Development. 2006. *The Economic Promise of Investing in High-Quality Preschool: Using Early Education to Improve Economic Growth and the Fiscal Sustainability of States and the Nation.* Washington, D.C.: CED.

Congressional Budget Office. 2004. *The Outlook for Social Security.* Washington D.C.: Government Printing Office. June.

Cost, Quality, and Child Outcomes Study Team. 1995. *Cost, Quality, and Child Outcomes in Child Care Centers.* 2nd edition. Denver, Colo.: University of Colorado Economics Department.

Courtney, Mark E. 1998. The costs of child protection in the context of welfare reform. *The Future of Children.* Vol. 8, No. 1, pp. 88-103. Spring.

Currie, Janet. 2001. Early childhood education programs. *Journal of Economic Perspectives*. Vol. 15, No. 2, pp. 213-38.

Currie, Janet, and Matthew Neidell. 2003. *Getting Inside the Black Box of Head Start Quality: What Matters and What Doesn't?* National Bureau of Economic Research, Working Paper #10091. Cambridge, Mass: NBER. November.

Currie, Janet, and Duncan Thomas. 1995. Does Head Start make a difference? *American Economic Review.* Vol. 85, No. 3, pp. 235-62. June.

Department for Education and Skills. 2006. *Provision for Children Under Five Years of Age in England: January 2006* (provisional). http://www.dfes.gsi.gov.uk.

Deutsch, Martin. 1967. *The Disadvantaged Child: Selected Papers of Martin Deutsch and Associates*. New York, N.Y: Basic Books.

Dickens, William T., Isabel Sawhill, and Jeffrey Tubbs. 2006. *The Effects of Investing in Early Education on Economic Growth*. Brookings Working Paper, Policy Brief #153. Washington, D.C.: The Brookings Institution.

Digest of Educational Statistics. 2004. Washington, D.C.: National Center for Education Statistics. http://nces.ed.gov.

Espinosa, Linda M. 2002. *High-Quality Preschool: Why We Need It and What It Looks Like*. National Institute for Early Education Research Policy Brief, Issue 1. New Brunswick, N.J.: NIEER. http://nieer.org/docs/index.php?DocID=58.

European Commission. 2002. *Key Data on Education in Europe, 2002.* Luxembourg: Office for Official Publications of the European Communities.

European Commission. 2005. *Key Data on Education in Europe, 2005,* Luxembourg: Office for Official Publications of the European Communities.

Foundation for Child Development. 2006a. *The Foundation for Child Development Child Well-Being Index (CWI), 1975-2004, With Projections for 2005: A Composite Index of Trends in the Well-Being of America's Children and Youth.* New York, N.Y.: FCD. http://www.soc.duke.edu/~cwi/.

Foundation for Child Development. 2006b. *The 2006 Foundation for Child Development Child Well-Being Index (CWI).* FCD Policy Brief series, No. 3. New York, N.Y.: FCD.

Garces, Eliana, Duncan Thomas, and Janet Currie. 2000. *Longer Term Effects of Head Start.* Working Paper, series 00-20. Santa Monica, Calif.: Rand Corporation.

Gelbach, Jonah B. 2002. Public schooling for young children and maternal labor supply. *American Economic Review.* Vol. 92, No. 1, pp.307-22.

Gilliam, Walter S., and Edward Zigler. 2001. A critical meta-analysis of all valuations of state-funded preschool from 1977 to 1998: Implications for policy, service delivery, and program evaluation. *Early Childhood Research Quarterly*. Vol. 15, No. 4, pp. 441-73.

Gilliam, Walter S., and Edward F. Zigler. 2004. *State Efforts to Evaluate the Effects of Prekindergarten: 1977 to 2003.* New Haven, Conn.: Yale University Child Study Center. http://nieer.org/docs/index.php?DocID=96.

Gormley, William T., and Ted Gayer. 2004. *The Effects of Universal Pre-K on Cognitive Development.* Washington, D.C.: Center for Research on Children in the U.S. Georgetown University. http://www.crocus.georgetown.edu.

Gormley, William T., and Ted Gayer. 2005. Promoting school readiness in Oklahoma: An evaluation of Tulsa's pre-k program. *The Journal of Human Resources*. Vol. 40, No.3.

Gormley, William T., Ted Gayer, Deborah Phillips, and Brittany Dawson. 2004. *The Effects of Oklahoma's Universal Pre-Kindergarten Program on School Readiness*. Washington, D.C.: Center for Research on Children in the U.S. Georgetown University. http://www.crocus.georgetown.edu.

Gormley, William T., and Deborah Phillips. The effects of universal pre-k in Oklahoma: Research highlights and policy implications. *Policy Studies Journal.* Forthcoming.

Graue, Elizabeth, Melissa A. Clements, Arthur J Reynolds, and Michael D. Niles. 2004. More than teacher directed or child initiated: Preschool curriculum type, parent involvement, and children's outcomes in the child-parent centers. *Education Policy Analysis Archive.* Vol. 12, No. 72.

Greenwood, Peter W., Karyn E. Model, C. Peter Rydell, and James Chiesa. 1998. *Diverting Children From a Life of Crime.* Santa Monica, Calif.: RAND Corporation, MR-699-1-UCB/RC/IF.

Greenwood, Peter W., C. Peter Rydell, Allan F. Abrahamse, Jonathan P. Caulkins, James Chiesa, Karyn E. Model, and Stephen P. Klein. 1994. *Three Strikes and You're Out: Estimated Benefits and Costs of California's New Mandatory-Sentencing Law.* Santa Monica, Calif.: Rand Corporation, MR-509-RC.

Hanushek, Eric A. 2002. *The Long-Run Importance of School Quality.* National Bureau of Economic Research. Working Paper No. 9071, Cambridge, Mass.: NBER.

Heckman, James. 1999. *Policies to Foster Human Development.* National Bureau of Economic Research Working Paper #7288. Cambridge, Mass.: NBER.

Heckman, James, and Alan Krueger. 2003. *Inequality in America: What Role for Human Capital Policies?* Cambridge, Mass: The MIT Press.

Heckman, James J., and Dimitriy V. Masterov. 2004. *The Productivity Argument for Investing in Young Children.* Working Paper 5. Washington, D.C.: Investing in Kids Working Group, Committee for Economic Development.

Helburn, Suzanne W., and Barbara R. Bergmann. 2002. *America's Child Care Problem: The Way Out.* New York, N.Y.: Palgrave.

Henry, Gary T., Craig S. Gordon, Laura W. Henderson, and Bentley D. Ponder. 2003. *Georgia Pre-K Longitudinal Study: Final Report 1996–2001.* Atlanta, Ga.: Georgia State University, Andrew Young School of Policy Studies. May.

Henry, Gary T., Laura W. Henderson, Bentley D. Ponder, Craig S. Gordon, Andrew J. Mashburn, and Dana K. Rickman. 2003. *Report of the Findings From the Early Childhood Study: 2001-02,* Atlanta, Ga.: Georgia State University, Andrew Young School of Policy Studies. August.

Henry, Gary T., Laura Henderson, and Bentley D. Ponder. 2004. *Ready or Not: A Snapshot of Children Entering Kindergarten in Georgia.* Atlanta, Ga.: Georgia State University, Andrew Young School of Policy Studies, Domestic Programs Office. September.

Henry, Gary T., Dana K Rickman, Bentley D. Ponder, Laura Henderson, Andrew Mashburn, and Craig S. Gordon. 2005. *The Georgia Early Childhood Study, 2001-2004: Final Report.* Atlanta, Ga.: Georgia State University, Andrew Young School of Policy Studies.

Hirsch Jr., E.D. 2004. *Equity Effects of Very Early Schooling in France.* Core Knowledge Preschool. http://www.coreknowledge.org/CKproto2/Preschool/FrenchEquity.htm.

Hovey, Kendra A., and Harold A. Hovey. 2006. *CQ's State Fact Finder 2006.* Washington D.C.: CQ Press.

Howes, C. 1988. Relations between early child care and schooling. *Developmental Psychology.* Vol. 24, pp. 53-7.

Institute for Taxation and Economic Policy. 2003. *Who Pays?* Washington, D.C.: ITEP.

Karoly, Lynn. 2001. "Investing in the Future: Reducing Poverty Through Human Capital Investments." In S. Danzigerand and Robert Haveman, eds., *Understanding Poverty.* Cambridge, Mass.: Harvard University Press.

Karoly, Lynn, and James H. Bigelow. 2005. *The Economics of Investing in Universal Preschool Education in California.* Santa Monica, Calif: Rand Corporation.

Karoly, Lynn, Peter Greenwood, Susan Everingham, Jill Hoube, Rebecca Kilburn, C. Peter Rydell, Matthew Sanders, and James Chiesa. 1998. *Investing in Our Children: What We Know and Don't Know About the Costs and Benefits of Early Childhood Interventions.* Washington, D.C.: Rand Corporation.

Karoly, Lynn, M. Rebecca Kilburn, James H. Bigelow, Jonathan P. Caulkins, and Jill S. Cannon. 2001. *Assessing Costs and Benefits of Early Childhood Intervention Programs: Overview and Application to the Starting Early Starting Smart Program.* Washington, D.C.: Rand Corporation.

Knudsen, Eric I., Heckman, James J., Cameron, Judy L., and Jack P. Shonkoff. 2006. *Economic, Neurobiological and Behavioral Perspectives on Building America's Future Workforce.* Working Paper 12298. Cambridge, Mass.: National Bureau of Economic Research.

Larsen, Jean M., and Clyde C. Robinson. 1989. Later effects of preschool on low-risk children. *Early Childhood Research Quarterly.* Vol. 4, pp. 133-44.

Lee, Valerie E., and David T. Burkam. 2002. *Inequality at the Starting Gate.*, Washington D.C.: Economic Policy Institute.

Levitt, Steven D., and Lance Lochner. 2000. "The Determinants of Juvenile Crime." In J. Gruber, ed., *Risky Behavior by Youths.* Chicago, Ill.: University of Chicago Press.

Lipps, G., and J. Yipton-Avila. 1999. *From Home to School: How Canadian Children Cope.* Culture, Tourism, and the Center for Education Statistics. Ottawa, Ontario: Statistics Canada. Catalogue # 89F0117XIE.

Love, John, Jeanne Brooks-Gunn, Diane Paulsell, and Allison Fuligni. 2002. *Making a Difference in the Lives of Infants and Toddlers and Their Families: The Impacts of Early Head Start.* Princeton, N.J.: Mathematica Policy Research, Inc.

Ludwig, Jens, and Douglas L. Miller. 2005. *Does Head Start Improve Children's Life Chances? Evidence From a Regression Discontinuity Design.* Working Paper 11702. Cambridge, Mass.: National Bureau of Economic Research.

Lynch, Robert G. 2004. *Exceptional Returns: Economic, Fiscal, and Social Benefits of Investment in Early Childhood Development.* Washington, D.C.: Economic Policy Institute.

Magnuson, Katherine A., Marcia K. Meyers, Christopher J. Ruhm, and Jane Waldfogel. 2004a. Inequality in preschool education and school readiness. *American Educational Research Journal.* Vol. 41, No. 1, pp. 115–57.

Magnuson, Katherine A., Christopher J. Ruhm, and Jane Waldfogel. 2004b. *Does Prekindergarten Improve School Preparation and Performance?* NBER Working Paper 10452, Cambridge, Mass.: National Bureau of Economic Research. April.

Magnuson, Katherine A., Marcia K. Meyers, Christopher J. Ruhm, and Jane Waldfogel. 2005. Inequality in children's school readiness and public funding. *Focus*. Vol. 24, No. 1, pp. 12-18. Fall.

Martin, Michael O., Ina V.S. Mullis, Eugenio J. Gonzalez, and Steven J. Chrostowski. 2004. *TIMSS 2003 International Science Report*. Boston, Mass.: Boston College, Lynch School of Education, TIMSS & PIRLS International Study Center.

Masse, Leonard, and W. Steven Barnett. 2002. A Benefit Cost Analysis of the Abecedarian Early Childhood Intervention. New Brunswick, N.J.: National Institute for Early Education Research, Rutgers University.

Miller, Ted R., Mark A. Cohen, and Brian Wiersema 1996. *Victim Costs and Consequences: A New Look*. Washington, D.C.: National Institute of Justice.

Miller, Ted R., Deborah A. Fisher, and Mark A. Cohen. 2001. Costs of juvenile violence: Policy implications. *Pediatrics*. Vol. 107, No. 1.

Mishel, Lawrence, Jared Bernstein, and Sylvia Allegretto. 2006. *The State of Working America 2006/2007*. An Economic Policy Institute book, Ithaca, N.Y.: ILR Press, an imprint of Cornell University Press.

Mocan, H. Naci, and Daniel I. Rees. 1999. *Economic Conditions, Deterrence and Juvenile Crime: Evidence from Micro Data*. National Bureau of Economic Reserarch Working Paper #7405. Cambridge Mass.: NBER.

Mullis, Ina V.S., Michael O. Martin, Albert E. Beaton, Eugenio J. Gonzalez, Dana L. Kelly, and Teresa A. Smith. 1998. *TIMSS 1995 Mathematics and Science Achievement in the Final Years of Secondary School: IEA's Third International Mathematics and Science Report*. Boston, Mass.: Boston College. TIMSS & PIRLS International Study Center, Lynch School of Education.

Mullis, Ina V.S., Michael O. Martin, Eugenio J. Gonzalez, and Steven J. Chrostowski. 2004. *TIMSS 2003 International Mathematics Report*. Boston, Mass.: Boston College. TIMSS & PIRLS International Study Center, Lynch School of Education.

Mullis, Ina V.S., Michael O. Martin, Eugenio J. Gonzalez, and Ann M. Kennedy. 2003. *PIRLS 2001 International Report: IEA's Study of Reading Literacy Achievement in Primary School in 35 Countries*. Boston, Mass.: Boston College. TIMSS & PIRLS International Study Center, Lynch School of Education.

National Institute for Child Health and Development. 2005. Early child care and children's development in the primary grades: Follow-up results from the NICHD study of early child care. *American Educational Research Journal*. Vol. 42, No.3, pp. 537-70.

Oden, S., L. J. Schweinhart, and D. P. Weikart. 2000. *Into Adulthood: A Study of the Effects of Head Start*. Ypsilanti, Mich.: High/Scope Press.

Olsen, Darcy, and Lisa Snell. 2006. *Assessing Proposals for Preschool and Kindergarten: Essential Information for Parents, Taxpayers and Policymakers*. Policy Study 344. Los Angeles, Calif.: Reason Public Policy Institute.

Organization for Economic Cooperation and Development. 2000. *Literacy in the Information Age: Final Report of the International Adult Literacy Survey*. Paris: OECD.

Organization for Economic Cooperation and Development. 2001. *Starting Strong: Early Childhood Education and Care.* Paris: OECD.

Organization for Economic Cooperation and Development. 2004. *Learning for Tomorrow's World: First Results from PISA 2003.* Paris: OECD.

Organization for Economic Cooperation and Development. 2006. *Labour Productivity Levels and GDP Per Capita.* OECD Productivity Database. Paris: OECD. January. http://www.oecd.org/dataoecd/28/17/36396820.xls

Parrish, Thomas, Jenifer Harr, Jean Wolman, Jennifer Anthony, Amy Merickel, and Phil Esra. 2004. *State Special Education Finance Systems, 1999-2000, Part II: Special Education Revenues and Expenditures*. Palo Alto, Calif.: Center for Special Education Finance, American Institutes for Research.

Peisner-Feinberg, E.S., Burchinal, M.R., Clifford, R.M., Culkin, M.L., Howes, C., and Kagan, S.L. 2001. The relation of preschool child-care quality to children's cognitive and social development trajectories through second grade. *Child Development*. Vol. 72, pp. 1534-53.

Phillips, D. A., M. Voran, E. Kisker, C. Howes, and M. Whitebook. 1994. Child care for children in poverty: opportunity or inequity? *Child Development*. Vol. 65, pp. 472-92.

Puma, Michael, Stephen Bell, Ronna Cook, Camoilla Heid, and Michael Lopez. 2005. *Head Start Impact Study: First Year Findings.* Washington D.C.: U.S. Department of Health and Human Services, Administration for Children and Families. May.

Reynolds, Arthur J. 1994a. Effects of a preschool plus follow-on intervention for children at risk. *Developmental Psychology.* Vol. 30, No. 6, pp. 787-804.

Reynolds, Arthur J. 1994b. One year of preschool intervention or two: Does it matter? *Early Childhood Research Quarterly.* Vol. 10, pp. 1-31.

Reynolds, Arthur J. 2000. *Success in Early Intervention: The Chicago Child-Parent Centers.* Lincoln, Neb.: University of Nebraska Press.

Reynolds, Arthur, Katherine Magnuson, and Suh-Ruu Ou. 2006. *PK-3 Education: Programs and Practices That Work in Children's First Decade*. Foundation for Child Development Working paper: Advancing PK-3, No. 6. New York, N.Y.: FCD.

Reynolds, Arthur J., Judy A. Temple, Dylan L. Robertson, and Emily A. Mann. 2001. Long-term effects of an early childhood intervention on educational achievement and juvenile arrest: A 15-year follow-up of low-income children in public schools. *Journal of the American Medical Association.* Vol. 285, No. 18, pp. 2339-46. May 9.

Reynolds, Arthur J., Judy A. Temple, Suh-Ruu Ou, Dylan L. Robertson, Joshua P. Mersky, James W. Topitzes, and Michael D. Niles. 2006. *Effects of a School-Based Early Childhood Intervention on Adult Health and Well-Being: A 20-Year Follow-up of Low-Income Families*. Early Childhood Research Collaborative Paper Series, August. http://www.earlychildhoodrc.org.

Reynolds, Arthur, Judy Temple, Dylan Robertson, and Emily Mann. 2002. Age 21 cost-benefit analysis of the Title 1 Chicago Child-Parent Centers. *Educational Evaluation and Policy Analysis*. Vol. 24, No. 4, pp. 267-303. Winter.

Ripple, C., W. Gilliam, N. Chanana, and E. Zigler. 1999. Will fifty cooks spoil the broth? *American Psychologist*. Vol. 54, No. 5, pp. 327-43.

Rolnick, Art, and Rob Grunewald. 2003. Early childhood development: Economic development with a high public return. *Fedgazette*. Federal Reserve Bank of Minneapolis. March.

Rothstein, Richard. 2004. *Class and Schools: Using Social, Economic, and Educational Reform to Close the Black-White Achievement Gap*. Washington, D.C.: Economic Policy Institute.

Sammons, P., K. Sylva, E. Melhuish, I. Siraj-Blatchford, B. Taggart, and K. Elliot. 2002. *Measuring the Impact of Preschool on Children's Cognitive Progress Over the Preschool Period.* Institute of Education Technical Paper 8a. London: University of London.

Sammons, P., K. Sylva, E. Melhuish, I. Siraj-Blatchford, B. Taggart, and K. Elliot. 2003. *Measuring the Impact of Preschool on Children's Social/Behavioral Development Over the Preschool Period.* Institute of Education Technical Paper 8b. London: University of London.

Schecter, C. 2002. *Language Growth in Low-Income Children in Economically Integrated Versus Segregated Preschool Programs.* West Hartford, Conn.: St. Joseph College.

Schulman, Karin, and W. Steven Barnett. 2005. *The Benefits of Prekindergarten for Middle-Income Children.* National Institute for Early Education Research Policy Report, New Brunswick, N.J.: NIEER.

Schweinhart, Lawrence. 1993. *Significant Benefits: The High/Scope Perry Preschool Study Through Age 27*. Ypsilanti, Mich.: High/Scope Educational Research Foundation.

Schweinhart, Lawrence. 2003 *Benefits, Costs, and Explanation of the High/Scope Perry Preschool Program.* Paper presented at the Meeting of the Society for Research in Child Development, Tampa, Florida, April 26.

Schweinhart, Lawrence J., Helen V. Barnes, and David P. Weikart, with W. Steven Barnett and Ann S. Epstein. 1993. *Significant Benefits: The High/Scope Perry Preschool Study Through Age 27.* Monograph No. 10. Ypsilanti, Mich.: High/Scope Educational Research Foundation.

Schweinhart, Lawrence J., Jeanne Montie, Zongping Xiang, W. Steven Barnett, Clive Belfield, and Milagros Nores. 2005. *Lifetime Effects: The High/Scope Perry Preschool Study Through Age 40*, Ypsilanti, Mich.: High/Scope Educational Research Foundation,

Schweke, William. 2004. *Smart Money: Education and Economic Development.* Washington, D.C.: Economic Policy Institute.

Scrivner, Scott, and Barbara Wolfe. 2003. *Universal Preschool: Much to Gain but Who Will Pay?* Institute for Research on Poverty. Discussion Paper No. 1271-03. Madison, Wisc.: University of Wisconsin-Madison, IRP.

Sedlak, Andrea, and Diane Broadhurst.1996. *The Third National Incidence Study of Child Abuse and Neglect (NIS-3).* U.S. Department of Health and Human Services, Administration for Children and Families, Administration on Children, Youth and Families, National Center on Child Abuse and Neglect. Washington, D.C.: Government Printing Office.

Smith, T., A. Kleiner, B. Parsad, E. Ferris, B. and Greene. 2003. *Prekindergarten in U.S. Public Schools, 2000-2001: Statistical Analysis Report.* Washington, D.C.: National Center for Education Statistics. (NCES 2003-019).

Snyder, H., C. Puzzanchera, and W. Kang. 2005. *Easy Access to FBI Arrest Statistics 1994-2002.* http://ojjdp.ncjrs.org/ojstabb/ezaucr/

Stahl, A., T. Finnegan, and W. Kang. 2005. *Easy Access to Juvenile Court Statistics 1985-2002.* http://ojjdp.ncjrs.org/ojstatbb/ezajcs/

State Policy Reports. 2006. K-12 education: Who pays how much? *Federal Funds Information for States*. Vol. 24, Issue 10. http://www.ffis.org

Stebbins, Helene, and Barbara Hanson Langford. 2006. *A Guide to Calculating the Cost of Quality Early Care and Education.* Washington, D.C.: The Finance Project.

Vandell, D.L., V.K. Henderson, and K.S. Wilson. 1988. A longitudinal study of children with daycare experiences of varying quality. *Child Development*, Vol. 59, pp. 1286-92.

UNICEF. 2005. *Child Poverty in Rich Countries 2005.* Innocenti Report Card No. 6. Florence, Italy: UNICEF Innocenti Research Centre.

U.S. Census Bureau. 2004a. *Projected Population of the United States, by Age and Sex: 2000 to 2050.* Washington, D.C.: Population Division, Population Projections Branch, U.S. Census Bureau. May 18.

U.S. Census Bureau. 2004b. *CPS Annual Demographic Survey.* Table PINC-04, March supplement, June 25. http://ferret.bls.census.gov/macro/032004/perinc/new04_000.htm.

U.S. Census Bureau. 2004c. *Current Population Survey*. Tables 1, 2, 3, 4, and 5. Washington, D.C.: U.S. Census Bureau. October.

U.S. Census Bureau. 2005. *Statistical Abstract of the United States*. Washington, D.C.: U.S. Census Bureau.

U.S. Department of Education, National Center for Education Statistics. 2005. Integrated Postsecondary Education, Data System (IPEDS). Washington, D.C.: U.S. Department of Education.

U.S. Department of Education, National Center for Education Statistics. 2006. *The Early Childhood Longitudinal Study, Kindergarten Class of 1998-99*. http://nces.ed.gov/ecls/

U.S. Department of Health and Human Services. 2004. *Child Maltreatment 2000.* Washington, D.C.: DHHS. http://www.acf.hhs.gov/programs/cb/publications/cmreports.htm.

U.S. Department of Health and Human Services. 2005a. *Foster Care FY 1999- FY 2003 Entries, Exits, and Numbers of Children in Foster Care on the Last Day of Each Federal Fiscal Year.* Washington, D.C.: DHHS, Administration for Children and Families, Adoption and Foster Care Analysis and Reporting System (AFCARS). April.

U.S. Department of Health and Human Services. 2005b. *Head Start Impact Study: First Year Findings*. Washington, D.C.: DHHS, Administration for Children and Families. May.

U.S. Department of Health and Human Services. 2005c. AFCARS Report # 7. Administration for Children and Families, Children's Bureau. www.acf.hhs.gov/programs/cb.

U.S. Department of Justice. 2006. *Justice Expenditure and Employment Extracts, 1992-2001.* Tables 1 and 3. Bureau of Justice Statistics. http://www.usdoj.gov/bjs/glance/tables/expogovtab.htm

Wolfe, Barbara, and Scott Scrivner. 2003. "Providing Universal Preschool for Four-Year-Olds," in Isabel Sawhill, ed., *One Percent for the Kids.* Washington, D.C.: Brookings Institution Press.

About the Author

Robert G. Lynch is the Everett E. Nuttle professor and chair of the Department of Economics at Washington College, where he has taught since 1998. Previously, he taught at the State University of New York at Cortland, where he served as chair of the department of economics from 1991 to 1993. His areas of specialization include public policy, public finance, international economics, economic development, and comparative economics. In the past, he has evaluated the adequacy and effectiveness of various state and local government economic policies, reviewed economic growth strategies, and analyzed the efficiency, fairness, and stability of state and local tax systems. Professor Lynch is also the author of several papers that have analyzed the effectiveness of state and local government economic policies in promoting economic development and creating jobs. He graduated with a B.A. degree in international and development economics from Georgetown University in 1979, earned a master's in economics from the State University of New York (SUNY) at Stony Brook in 1981, and received a Ph.D. in economics from SUNY Stony Brook in 1984.

His most recent books for the Economic Policy Institute were *Rethinking Growth Strategies—How State and Local taxes and Services Affect Economic Development* (2004) and *Exceptional Returns—Economic, Fiscal, and Social Benefits of Investment in Early Childhood Development* (2004).

About EPI

The Economic Policy Institute was founded in 1986 to widen the debate about policies to achieve healthy economic growth, prosperity, and opportunity. Today, despite rapid growth in the U.S. economy in the latter part of the 1990s, inequality in wealth, wages, and income remains historically high. Expanding global competition, changes in the nature of work, and rapid technological advances are altering economic reality. Yet many of our policies, attitudes, and institutions are based on assumptions that no longer reflect real world conditions.

With the support of leaders from labor, business, and the foundation world, the Institute has sponsored research and public discussion of a wide variety of topics: globalization; fiscal policy; trends in wages, incomes, and prices; education; the causes of the productivity slowdown; labor market problems; rural and urban policies; inflation; state-level economic development strategies; comparative international economic performance; and studies of the overall health of the U.S. manufacturing sector and of specific key industries.

The Institute works with a growing network of innovative economists and other social-science researchers in universities and research centers all over the country who are willing to go beyond the conventional wisdom in considering strategies for public policy. Founding scholars of the Institute include Jeff Faux, former EPI president; Lester Thurow, Sloan School of Management, MIT; Ray Marshall, former U.S. secretary of labor, professor at the LBJ School of Public Affairs, University of Texas; Barry Bluestone, Northeastern University; Robert Reich, former U.S. secretary of labor; and Robert Kuttner, author, editor of *The American Prospect*, and columnist for *Business Week* and the *Washington Post* Writers Group.

For additional information about the Institute, contact EPI at 1333 H St. NW, Suite 300, Washington, DC 20005, (202) 775-8810, or visit www.epi.org.

OTHER BOOKS FROM THE ECONOMIC POLICY INSTITUTE

Exceptional Returns
Economic, Fiscal, and Social Benefits of Investement in Early Childhood Development
by Robert Lynch

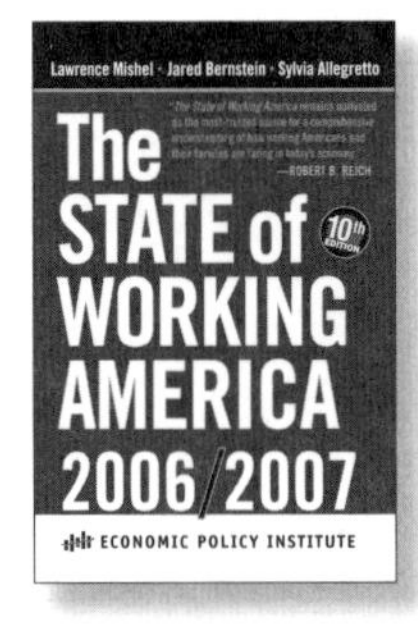

The State of Working America 2006/2007
by Lawrence Mishel, Jared Bernstein, and Sylvia Allegretto

Rethinking High School Graduation Rates and Trends
by Lawrence Mishel and Joydeep Roy

Class and Schools
Using Social, Economic, and Educational Reform to Close the Black-White Achievement Gap
by Richard Rothstein

The Charter School Dust-Up
Examining the Evidence on Enrollment and Achievement
by Martin Carnoy, Rebecca Jacobsen, Lawrence Mishel, and Richard Rothstein

Smart Money
Education and economic development
by William Schweke

Order these and other EPI books at **www.epi.org**